Black Women's Narratives of NHS Work-Based Learning: An Ethnodrama

Black Women's Narratives of NHS Work-Based Learning: An Ethnodrama

The Difference between Rhetoric and Lived Experience

Peggy P. Warren

PETER LANG

Oxford · Bern · Berlin · Bruxelles · New York · Wien

Bibliographic information published by Die Deutsche Nationalbibliothek.
Die Deutsche Nationalbibliothek lists this publication in the Deutsche
Nationalbibliografie; detailed bibliographic data is available on the Internet at
http://dnb.d-nb.de.

A catalogue record for this book is available from the British Library.

A CIP catalog record for this book has been applied for at the Library of Congress.

Cover image: Returning to move forward. By T. T. Taylor.

ISBN 978-1-78997-462-1 (print) • ISBN 978-1-78997-463-8 (ePDF)
ISBN 978-1-78997-464-5 (ePub) • ISBN 978-1-78997-465-2 (mobi)

© Peter Lang AG 2019

Published by Peter Lang Ltd, International Academic Publishers,
52 St Giles, Oxford, OX1 3LU, United Kingdom
oxford@peterlang.com, www.peterlang.com

Peggy P. Warren has asserted her right under the Copyright, Designs and Patents Act,
1988, to be identified as Author of this Work.

All rights reserved.
All parts of this publication are protected by copyright.
Any utilisation outside the strict limits of the copyright law, without
the permission of the publisher, is forbidden and liable to prosecution.
This applies in particular to reproductions, translations, microfilming,
and storage and processing in electronic retrieval systems.

Printed in Germany

This book is dedicated to my father, Vincent Charles Warren, who showed me that reaching down to impact another human being was as important as, if not more important than, reaching up for myself. My 'world' is the way it is because of his grounding. He raised a daughter who is 'likkle but tallawa.' Major, as we affectionately call him, will always be my number 1 superhero and inspiration.

To my brothers, Bill, Tony and Butto – what journeys! From Birmingham to Jamaica to meet Meger, Bredda, Dawn, Maureen, Paulette and Gee, then back to Britain to join the NHS, Longbridge and the armed forces. Stories and life lessons from our youth will keep us laughing 'til we're old and grey.

To my mother Cissy, your generous heart means you'll never be alone.

To my best friend Sister White, every important step I've taken in the last three decades you've been there with and for me.

I would not be who I am today without all of you.

Thank you.

Contents

List of figures	ix
Foreword	xi
Preface	xv
Acknowledgements	xvii
List of abbreviations	xix
Introduction	1
List of main characters	7
Scenes of the ethnodrama	9

SCENE 1
The dreamers in Jamaica heading for the motherland 11

SCENE 2
Black women, it's time to break the silence 15

SCENE 3
We really wanted to be nurses 19

SCENE 4
Getting to grips with power 33

SCENE 5
Did anyone think this through? 43

SCENE 6
If only we had known 51

SCENE 7
Bittersweet realisation – hope we are the last 83

SCENE 8
Sankofa's reflection and guidance 109

Postscript 115

Bibliography 117

Index 121

Figures

Figure 1.	Nsoromma – Banking model of education.	91
Figure 2.	NSAA – Education and work did not uplift me.	91
Figure 3.	Sumsum – No affective education.	92
Figure 4.	GyeNyame – Education that oppresses.	92
Figure 5.	Bese Saka – Educated to regress.	93
Figure 6.	Aroma – Rethinking educational failure.	93
Figure 7.	Aya – Education uplifts self esteem.	94
Figure 8.	Matie Masie – Time poor education doesn't work.	94
Figure 9.	Dame Dame – We were not given student status.	95
Figure 10.	Akoben – Education struggle and breakthrough.	95

Foreword

This is a truly important book of relevance to all those working towards racial justice in the NHS and beyond. It describes Black women's trajectories of work-based learning in the NHS from their perspectives, using their voices. It goes beyond simpler notions of understanding 'lived experience' as it presents their relived trajectories of extending their thinking, transforming their understanding and rethinking their possibilities. There are painful, moving accounts of oppression, disrespect and devaluing. It hurts to read some of the scenes. However, this is also a story of the heartwarming, inspirational, transformational relationships amongst Black women striving to change their life chances, as well as those of their wider families and communities. It is an inspirational read!

Black Women's Narratives of NHS Work-based Learning – An Ethnodrama is as engaging as the best of novels. Simultaneously, it is a beautiful vehicle for understanding the self and others in relation to a colonial exercise of 'power over'. Dr Peggy P. Warren has crafted classical academic data artistically, rendering this book accessible to many who would not typically engage with such a work. It meets, surpasses and transcends the requirements of academia. This book stands as a rich source of information, paradigm-shifting conception, new imaginings and decolonising possibilities. Drawing upon traditional, liberational and cultural traditions, the scenes are deeply educational as they delightfully and elegantly expound the women's embedded and embodied ways of knowing.

These women's experiences are, in many ways, a microcosm of the experiences of Black people throughout the NHS. For the wider system, it demonstrates how having good intentions without deep understanding is not enough. In the absence of committed, reflexive partnerships that transform aspirations and skills into reward systems, affective pedagogy and notions of a redefined organisational identity, nothing will change! The promises of equality all too often lead to fruitless activity that breaks hearts as it fails to deliver.

These women are not passive victims, but rich, resilient characters struggling to progress in the face of resistance whilst understanding that to progress, they need to learn much more than the content of the curriculum they are presented with. From the promise-filled rhetoric of widening participation policies linked to 'upskilling and progression', they experienced behaviours, practices and beliefs that denied and betrayed their aspirations and their humanity. What these courageous women expose through interrogating their experiences is of huge value to all those committed to addressing issues of racial inequality in the NHS and beyond.

This book highlights the need for Black (and other 'non-traditional') learners, to critically engage with education and development 'opportunities', and not submit naively to a process that compounds and reinforces their devalued realities. For them to engage critically, they need to have a narrative that effectively counters the dominant one. For them to have that narrative, they need to understand how racism and colonialism permeate unconscious (and conscious) societal processes. These processes result in a denial of their professional, social, educational, psychological and economic development. They need to underpin that narrative with knowledge of their pre-colonial civilisations and their significant and foundational contributions to human civilisation. They need to engage with the writings of the women and men who have studied and theorised strategies most capable of supporting Black progress in an often politely hostile organisational context. The message is clear for people from 'non-traditional' backgrounds; depending on the system without an informed critical perspective leaves one vulnerable to psychic damage.

This is a culturally vibrant book viewed through epistemic lens and motivated by relational ethics of care. As a narrative inquiry, it reflects a respectful collaboration between those who strive for basic progression in organisations and those who have achieved academic positions. Critical, self-reflexive conversations in safe places led both groups to 'out' their shared experiences of racism and institutional barriers to their professional progression. The message is again very clear: we can learn to love each other and strategise together in order to achieve the outcomes we deserve.

Foreword

Every Black person, every agent of change, every woman, every leader, every educator, everyone in the NHS needs to read this book.

Eden Charles PhD
Chief Executive & Managing Consultant
People Opportunities Limited
8 May 2019

Preface

> When talking about their lives, people lie sometimes, forget a lot, exaggerate, become confused and get things wrong. Yet, they are revealing truths. These truths don't reveal the past 'as it actually was' spiriting to a standard of objectivity. They give us instead the truths of our experiences. Unlike the reassuring truth of scientific ideal, the truths of personal narrative are neither open to proof or self-evident.
> — Personal Narratives Group (1989: 261)

Since 2010, the National Health Service (NHS) has set out new models of care and care strategies. Amongst them was the introduction of the Assistant Practitioner (AP), a new ancillary role that a qualified nurse could delegate clinical work to. This book examines and centralises the experiences of ten Black British and Black Caribbean women's experiences of the foundation degree (fd) programme that promised to lead to the AP role and its impact on their personal and professional identities. It (re)tells, (re)captures and (re)presents their accounts of higher education. Black Feminist Methodological Stance is put to work to centre and privilege Black women who transitioned through the research process unearthing, examining and unapologetically speaking their 'truths'.

The analysis is intentionally theoretically provocative and uses performative autoethnograpy to present the voices of the women through characters in fictional settings. The characters use the works of predominantly Black philosophers to critically reflect on their experiences of education. Their exposures to philosophies leads them to Black feminist epistemologies. This book demands engagement; it challenges all who read it to come and reside in the women's spaces ... to feel the discomforts ... to rethink the stereotypes ... to speak of the biases ... then to co-align with women like these to make the NHS truly inclusive ... it questions ... challenges ... and seeks honest approaches to fairness in nursing education and the NHS more generally.

This book breaks the silence of Black women in the NHS and makes the theorised assertion of our 'right to write' as Black women about Black women and for Black women. The presentation of the stories as performance autoethnography renders this book accessible, as well as significant and important for academic scholarship. It resists making recommendations that are ineffective liberatory tools of the master's house and that fail to make a difference for Black women in assigned subordinated spaces. Finally, this work challenges Black women in the NHS to engage in activism for their own professional emancipation.

Acknowledgements

I would like to acknowledge God, who purposes each of his creation, who I choose to align with as I strive to make my small 'world' a little fairer than it was when I joined it.

To the ten amazingly courageous and resilient Black women whose stories made this book possible, I salute you! I am indebted to you for your willingness to share, baring so many of your experiences that had never been told. You made this book possible. My hope is that your experiences of pain, disappointment and injustices, as well as your accounts of overcoming, your pride and your resilience, will contribute to more positive educational experiences for future generations of Black people working in the NHS.

L. A. Lawson, my superbly broadminded sounding block, thank you for the multiple hours you invested in listening, as I tested out my private thoughts before I 'outed' them on paper. You are a dependable friend and I appreciate you.

Dr Eden Charles, thank you for taking time out of your incredibly busy schedule to read this book and write the foreword. From our very first conversation, you told me you believed in me and I'm totally humbled by your support for this book. You are truly inspirational.

Thanks to Professor Alex Kendall and the late Professor Joyce Canaan, who supported and encouraged me to take risks and write in a way that was true to me.

To T. T. Taylor, for giving me the permission to use his artwork for the front cover of this book.

Finally, to Sister Richards and Sister Rose, my octogenarian anchors. I am so very blest by your continued love and care; you are undoubtedly the wind beneath my wings.

Abbreviations

ACE	Active Centralised Empowerment
AP	Assistant Practitioner
BB	Black British
BBC	British Broadcasting Association
BC	Black Caribbean
BFMS	Black Feminist Methodological Stance
BME	Black Minority Ethnic
CEO	Chief Executive Officer
ESN	Educationally Sub Normal
FD	Foundation Degree
GNC	General Nursing Council
HCA	Health Care Assistant
HE	Higher Education
HEI	Higher Education Institution
ICT	Information Computer Technology
MA	Masters of Arts
NHS	National Health Service
NMC	Nursing and Midwifery Council
RCN	Royal College of Nursing
SEN	State Enrolled Nurse
SRN	State Registered Nurse
TAP	Trainee Assistant Practitioner
UK	United Kingdom
UNESCO	United Nations Educational Scientific and Cultural Organisations
USA	United States of America
WP	Widening Participation
WPL	Work Place Learning

Introduction

I decided to write this book following three separate but interrelated life occurrences. First, my determination to teach from the standpoint that education should be life-transforming. My approach to teaching has been influenced by the works of bell hooks, Audre Lorde, W. E. B. Dubois, Paulo Freire, Booker T. Washington and others who advocate that, for education to be meaningful, it must be a reciprocal process that leads to social or economic liberation for oppressed groups.

Secondly, the puzzling professional regression of some of my Black British and Black Caribbean mature colleagues. Let me explain. Several women working in low-skilled, low-paid roles in the NHS demonstrated their competence to access higher education (HE) and shared with me, and others, their aspirations to engage in professional development. However, over half of the Black British and Black Caribbean women who commenced a part-time, two-year foundation degree (fd) in Health and Social Care 'failed' to gain the full qualification.

Finally, my confusion about these 'failures' coincided with a visit I made to Ghana in 2008. On the side of a very busy street in Accra, I met an elderly woman who was a stranger to me. This stranger told me little things about myself, for example, my Akan name was the day I was born, and she was resolute that she could direct me to the village of my ancestors. Observing my confusion, exasperatedly, she dismissed me with the Akan word, 'Sankofa'. 'Sankofa' literally means: 'return to the past, learn from it and move forward'. Since then, I have embraced the spirit of Sankofa and used the Sankofa concept, especially when it came to trying to make sense of what was happening to my Black British and Black Caribbean colleagues as students in the National Health Service.

Reclaiming oral histories and methodologies

Black women in low-skilled and low-paid roles in the NHS are generally muted, their voices are not represented in the dominant discourses within the health sector and on the very rare occasions they are represented, they generally have others speaking for them. This book centralises the voices of Black British and Black Caribbean women.

The contributors to this book are adult children of post-war Jamaican immigrants to Britain. Our parents arrived in the UK predominantly by invitation through recruitment drives. The 'cry for help' from the colonies was to join the British in rebuilding the 'motherland', which would prove beneficial for immigrants too, as it would enable them to gain a better standard of life for themselves, as well as secure a 'prosperous future' for their children.

Nursing education experienced by Black women in the present age is captured quite accurately by Imbo (2001), who described education under colonialism: it is not neutral, but rather a way of transferring colonial countries' dominant modes of knowledge production. Woodson (1933), Fanon (1967) and Dubois (1973) argue that the presentation of education deemed appropriate for Blacks was 'contradictory' to their traditional practices because the oral conveying was discredited, giving legitimacy to written literature. In academic work, orally conveyed works are considered subordinate to written literature, but I have included oral accounts as a means of resisting the colonial hegemony which dictates how literature is defined and in so doing relegates important aspects of my Black cultural epistemology. In this book, the oral accounts are given the same level of importance and acknowledgement as the written accounts. This small-'p' political work aims to be 'culturally true' and, for me, that includes verbatim reproductions of accounts in which the women used Jamaican patois. The reader will find that Black women's conversations are generally more circular than the linear format of written text. Tuwe (2016) offers an insight into the 'circular' way of telling when he states:

> Our stories offer explanations of natural phenomena, teach moral values, provide us with a sense of identity and are entertaining as well as instructive. Storytellers repeat

words, phrases, gestures and verses or stanzas ... the audience actively participates as they learn important aspects of their culture ... storytelling is a mode for preserving our history and traditional culture. (pp. 2–3)

Oral storytelling is an integral aspect of my culture's way of disseminating and cascading information. Black feminist stance provided the framework to centre and privilege the everyday lived experiences of ten Black women as significant and important data for academic scholarship. Boylorn (2016) argues that:

> there are some potential challenges for black women primarily studying their own lives as they will have biases that could influence their interpretations. In addition, we may dismiss or overlook important information or findings, because we perceive it to be normal and not out of the ordinary. It is also possible that we disregard important details. (p. 359)

I acknowledge my biases and assert that this book is very much a partial retelling of our lived experiences.

Black feminist standpoint as a theoretical framework synchronises well with performance autoethnography. The value of this methodological blending is asserted by Boylorn (2016):

> Autoethnography, coupled with black feminist stance, provides an opportunity for black women to embrace their truth, examine their lived experiences through a cultural lens using creative writing techniques and research methods to situate, interrogate and critique our experiences while making sense of cultural phenomena. When autoethnography came into the picture it made sense in the context of my black feminist politics. (p. 74)

The prodigious contribution Black women have made and continue to make in Britain's NHS is uncontested (Jones and Snow, 2010). Black student nurses from the 1950s to the 1980s were generally categorised using 'the deficit theory model'. The 'deficit theory model' of education suggests that Black people are academically deficient and education interventions should correct the deficiencies.

As an educator with decades of teaching experience in a range of educational contexts both in the UK and overseas, I became suspicious of, as well as frustrated by, Britain's reliance on the 'deficit theory model' to explain both the educational and professional underachievement of 'people like me'. Britain's nursing education history – the little that makes any reference to Blacks – generally gives the impression that our mothers were incapable of achieving the higher nursing qualification, which became the justification for Black women being significantly over-represented in the subordinate State Enrolled Nurse (SEN) position of the UK's nursing hierarchy (Carter 1998, Kramer 2006 and Jones and Snow 2010). The authors referenced discuss the complexities, injustices and exploitations of immigrant, Black women's labour.

The UK's nursing education model shift was introduced in the Queen's speech of 1978. This included a move from a solitary apprenticeship model governed by the General Nursing Council (GNC) in hospitals, to incorporate work placements in hospitals with theory taught in higher education institutions (HEIs). This new approach meant that the certificate in nursing was replaced by a diploma for most, though a degree route was also available. Significantly, the student nurse was given trainee status and therefore had to be supernumerary to the shift team. In 2013, the diploma route was also abolished and nursing became a solely graduate profession.

Like many of the issues affecting Black women in nursing, the end of the SEN role and its impact on Black nurses has not been discussed much in nursing literature. Baxter (1998) argued that the Black SENs' career progression was in the power of the dominant group who had for decades restricted them to subordinated and peripheral spaces in the NHS. Baxter (1998) asserts:

> it is only through an instinct for survival that many younger enrolled nurses felt the need to take up the conversion courses finally leading to registration ... however, the opportunity to undertake the conversion courses was dependent on recommendations and references from ward sisters and managers. (p. 29)

On gaining registration, Black women found themselves fighting structures which appeared invisible to everyone but them. Hill Collins (1991) describes their experience thus:

> even when the political and economic conditions that originally generated controlling images disappear, such images prove remarkably tenacious because they not only

> keep Black women oppressed but are key in maintaining interlocking systems of race, class and gender oppression. (p. 68)

Hill Collins' (1991) words reinforce the urgency to engage with my past. Not to become a victim of it, but to proactively encourage Black women to critically engage and scrutinise our situations using our histories. Primarily because it is through knowing our histories that Black women realise that we may have internalised stereotypes of ourselves, therefore potentially becoming effective conduits for perpetuating our own oppression.

This book highlights the challenges that come with so-called widening participation opportunities. It provides insights into educational experiences of Black women working in Britain's 'National Treasure'. This book is a genuine inquiry into the lived experiences of Black women with the intention of making sense of our educational journeys and doing so in such a way that others can learn from them, critique them, contribute to them and share them.

List of main characters

Pseudonyms include African Adinkra symbols, which capture each woman's characteristics.

Bese Saka		This symbol signifies economic wellbeing, affluence and authority over other people and nations.
Mate Masie		This symbol teaches the importance of imbibing all forms of information prudently in order to acquire wisdom and knowledge.
Nsoromma		This symbol reminds people to regard God as their father and encourages a sense of confidence and reliability.
Nsaa		This symbol signifies that quality and durability should be a hall mark in their productivity.
Akoma		This symbol teaches the importance of tolerance in the face of provocation.
Aya		This symbol teaches that life is full if uncertainty, therefore the survival of mankind requires strong will to face all challenges.
SunSum		This is a symbol of spiritually.
Akoben		This symbol signifies alertness and readiness to serve a good cause.
GyeNyame		This symbol reflects the supremacy, power and domination of over all situations and creations.

Dame-Dame	This symbol encourages the exercising of the brain in order for it to be reactivated.
Sankofa	This symbol teaches wisdom in learning from the past which helps building the future. It teaches people to cherish and value their culture and avoid its adulteration.
Mama B (Sepo)	This symbol encourages freedom of speech, but disallows speeches which bring about strife.
Mmara-Krado	This symbol signifies supreme authority, justice and equality of everybody before the law.
Owo Foro Adobe	This symbol signifies steadfastness, prudence and diligence.
Akoko Nan	This symbol represents the parental role and signifies protection and correction.

Scenes of the ethnodrama

Scene 1. The dreamers in Jamaica heading for the motherland
Jamaica, 14 February 1948
The performance commences in a fictional setting in Jamaica. The characters would have been from what we now call 'the Windrush generation' giving oral accounts of migrating to the motherland.

Scene 2. Black women, it's time to break the silence
This scene introduces a safe space for self-introduction and insights into parents' employment in the UK. It also provides insights into the characters' educational legacies.

Scene 3. We really wanted to be nurses
Here the women discuss their ambitions to become nurses. They share their belief that a foundation degree was going to get their foot in the door. They agree on their personal commitment to using a Black woman's way of knowing as an approach to their self-education.

Scene 4. Getting to grips with power
The women agree to the use of the Centralised Empowerment approach. They are challenged by Mama B to consider the 'power relations' of their educational experiences. They reflect use theory to explore key ways of making mature students feel safe in universities.

Scene 5. Did anyone think this through?
NHS England's Conference – 27 July 2013 – The Drum, Birmingham

A verbatim interview with a member of a commissioning team. The venue and date of the conference are fictional. The Drum was a Birmingham Arts venue predominantly used by the Black community until its closure in June 2016.

Scene 6.   If only we had known
A Black feminist epistemological session incorporating the characters' evocative reflections and responses to the commissioner's interview, along with a reflection on their principal areas of support and how they built resilience. Much questioning of the self.

Scene 7.   Bittersweet realisation – hope we are the last
The final formal meeting introduces a range of teaching approaches, cathartic singing of Bob Marley's 'Redemption Song' and a keynote speaker, Dr Owo Adobe. The women send messages to self then ask questions of the university, the course funders, the workplace and finally aspirational Black mature students.

Scene 8.   Sankofa's reflections and guidance
Sankofa dialogues with an ancestral spirit, Akoko Nan. In keeping with her name, she revisits literature and critically questions the education experience. She plans to leave their stories as lessons for future generations.

SCENE 1

The dreamers in Jamaica heading for the motherland

Jamaica, 14 February 1948

On the sandy beach of Negril under the scorching sun, eight hopeful couples and two single men are discussing their future dreams. Though the motherlan' has been at war and times are hard, the earth still produces food for survival. Saltfish is sparse but they clubbed together their rations to get enough food to bring and share. Yam and saltfish are buried beneath the hot coals in de sand. The redemptive lyrics of reggae music invigorates the dreamers. Motherlan' calls and the pull is 'trong. As the gossip goes, motherlan' streets are paved with gold. The men lie face down on the beach, in unison they repeat the common dream that Ganja man has written in the sand:

'We go, we earn, we learn, we return.'

Reggae beats are followed by the ballads of the blues. Brooke Benton, Ella Fitzgerald and Sam Cooke are amongst the great musical storytellers. Each story resonates with someone in the group. As the ballads resound, the men rise and 'drop foot'. The women look on and giggle. Everyone's happy. In the ice box is cool aid, rum punch, Dragon stout and Red Stripe beer.

The beer-filled men seem to unanimously agree that, for them, migration would be a win-win venture. The motherlan' gets her labourers, and we get work to help us escape the employment and education limitations of the colonial island.

Rupie: 'Well, if I go to Englan', I can buy some land back here.'
Cyrus: (Chips in.) 'I would love to build a house fi miself too.'

Zekey: (Pipes up.) 'You know something, I always dream that one day I would travel and further my education. I'm an electrician now, but I would like to get into engineering and build something that I would be remembered for.'

Ganja man: (Taps Zekey on the back.) 'Forever the dreamer eh Zekey?'

At the point of Ganja man's utterance, the women re-converge.

Jackie: 'Hey there Mr Dreamer, you wanna know what I dream 'bout? That I will go to Englan' an' train to be a nurse. Mi a go hab four pickney who will all speak prop-a-lee. You know, like the daughters of the king.'

Evelyn: 'Yeah girl, mi wid yo'. I wan' be a nurse, bringing healing and health to the sick and wounded of Englan'. Mi a go marries a nice man an' have t'ree sons. Mi wi groom mi son dem fi love education. Dem wi get big job inna Englan'. An a dem a go be mi pension'.

Laughter erupts. The women walk away to check the food. From beneath the sand rises the aroma of roasted sal'fish and yam carried by the sea breeze.

Jackie: 'Uno cum get uno food, an' no meck mi haffi call uno again'.

The men singe the banana leaves they carried from 'country' over the charred coals to make plates. The women stand in line mimicking the quaint British accents they hear on the British Broadcasting Corporation (BBC). As each woman collects her food she curtsies and giggles. Together they sit in a circle on the sand, food on laps, drinks by their sides. Each woman takes turns in sharing her vision of working as equals amongst white women in de motherlan'.

Ida: 'Huh, this is no joke, we better practise hour best 'nglish 'cause I've got mi letter from de British 'ospital.'

(Then, with much excitement, there is an echoing ...)

Jackie: 'Me to.'
Evelyn: 'Me to.'

The dreamers in Jamaica heading for the motherland

(Cutie was quiet, so the women turn to face her expecting an explanation.)

Cutie: (Gingerly.) 'So have I.'

Ida, the loudest of the group, stands up, slaps her thigh and starts a jig.

Ida: 'Hell a pop ... we a go a Englan' fi true'.

Meanwhile, the men tame the fire water (white rum) with ginger beer and soda water. The sea breeze caresses their faces and carries the hubbub of chatter and laughter.

Denzil and Zekey under their liquor talk about getting with white women. These two, as the saying on the island goes, are young, free and single. Fearing the wrath of the women there present, Zekey stares directly at Denzil as he speaks.

Zekey: 'Mi hear sey de white 'oman dem love black man, cause dem into tropical loving'.
Denzil: (Responds at the top of his voice.) 'If dem hear so, dem hear right. Dem know sey we be lover men'. (Jiving his hips whilst struggling to stay on his feet.)

The women glare; that's all it took. Denzil and Zekey try to teck dem foot in dem han' but they can hardly stand, much less run. They fall flat on their faces in the sand. Laughter erupts and all is well again. As the group board the bus for home, the ghetto-blaster belts out Jimmy Rushing blues.

Over six decades later, the daughters of the Negril beach dreamers are all living in England and working in the NHS in the Midlands. Denzil and Zekey married a Scottish lassie and an English rose respectively.

The twenty-first-century NHS transformation agenda created opportunities for those working in low-skilled, low-paid roles to undertake Widening Participation (WP) educational opportunities. As a result, a Midlands Trust internally advertised opportunities for allied health professionals working in Band 2 roles to undertake 'Band 4' training which would result in a promotion and a salary increase from *Band 2 – £15,251 –£17,978* to *Band 4, £19,217–£22,458*.

The new foundation degree (fd) was a two-year undergraduate programme delivered through a local university, with clinical skills developed and practised through work-based learning. Overall, the failure to complete rate was quite high. Sankofa, was curious to explore why a significant number of her Black colleagues had 'failed' to complete the two-year programme. She had a vested interest. As a work-based educator, she had taught those who 'failed' to complete and in several cases relationships with the women had transitioned from colleagues to friends.

SCENE 2

Black women, it's time to break the silence

At noon, on a very chilly November day in 2012, a group of mature Black women converge in a community room in Handsworth, Birmingham. The room is large with oversized radiators which effectively keep the chills at bay. Scattered around the room are comfy chairs. There is a small kitchenette to the left of the room. Before long the women are active in the kitchenette. Microwaves are pinging and the contents of the microwaves exude a plethora of fragrances from Caribbean cuisines. There is an array of Chicken: jerked, stewed and fried systematically placed on the worktop. Piping hot rice boiled with coconut milk is steaming in Pyrex bowls. On foil trays are giant fried dumplings and in a Tupperware bowl next to the dumplings is Caribbean coleslaw.

Punch is poured from bottles and jugs. One punch has J. Wray and Nephew rum (fire wata), alongside it is a second jug with punch for the drivers, the lightweights and the faithful.

Scattered around the room are: Bese Saka aged 47, Mate Masie 50, Nsoromma 38, Nsaa 41, Akoma 50, Aya 41, SunSum 50, Akoben 51, GyeNyame 45, Dame-Dame 48 and Sankofa 45. Between them, they have given a prodigious fourteen decades and four years' service to the NHS in the UK. The academic supporting the women in their Black feminist epistemological search is Mama B.

Mama B: (Stands tall and authoritatively summons.)
'Alright ladies, teck uno food and come and jain we inna de circle. Uno no badda meck mi haffi call uno again'.

The women hurriedly assemble the seats into a smaller, more intimate circle. They snatch their plates and sit with food on laps and drinks at their feet.

Sankofa: 'Okay everyone, let us start culturally. Firstly, as our parents taught us, let's bless the food and the time we're going to spend together. GyeNyame, will you do the honours?'

Akoben:	'Meck it shart, GyeNyame, ar' else mi a start 'it, faar mi caan 'it de col' food'.

The women in chorus: 'Amen'. (There's pointing in Akoben's direction and giggling.)

GyeNyame:	(Ignores the laughter.) 'Oh father God in Heaven, please bless this food to our bodies and bless the 'ands that prepare it, I hope them was clean (chuckle) and bless our time together. Amen. Short enough Akoben?'
Akoben:	'No bad, no bad at all ... mi nah sey nuttun bout de clean 'ands'.
Sankofa:	(Walks to the centre of the circle.) 'Alright, Akoben ... done now! We from the African diaspora generally honour the ancestors when we congregate but let's bring it a little closer this afternoon and honour our parents. Each one will recognise their start, however humble, 'cause as they use to tell us; it's not how you start, it's how you finish. I'll start ... today I honour my part-Cuban/part-Jamaican mother and my part-Irish/part-Ghanaian/Jamaican father. My dad, a "professor of life" worked as an ambulance driver here in England. My mother was a factory worker. For their lives and contributions to humanity, I give thanks ... Who's next?'
Bese Saka:	'I give t'anks and praise for my parents who both came here from sunny Jamaica. Daddy did factory work and mummy was an auxiliary nurse ... Gwaan, MM'.
Mate Masie:	'A sending out spiritual vibes to mum and dad, from Jamaica. Mum was a seamstress and my darling dad was an electrician ... teck it from yasso, N.'
Nsoromma:	'I'm going to mix it up a little bit, dearly departed Jamaican dad ... you worked hard on the British trains. I just wanna say, you left too soon, but when you left, I found my voice. I thank you for that. My beautiful mum from Scotland, no one makes a bouquet like you do, you bring fragrance and beauty wherever you go ... follow that, Nsaa.'
Nsaa:	(Laughing.) 'Well girl, it's not just you mixing it up. You know the Jamaican Motto: "Out of many, one people". One also brings diversity. Daddy was an electrician, a petite bourgeois, from Jamaica and mother, the English Rose worked in a factory. I honour you both for your values and love.'
Akoma:	'Today, I honour the absent father from the island where rum flows and music weaves us through our past, present and provides signs for our future. A mother who came to Britain, from Jamaica, who worked as an auxiliary nurse, then converted to a mental health nurse. Big up your resilience, ma'am ... Go, Aya.'

Black women, it's time to break the silence

Aya:	'I'm going to honour Jamaica for producing two beautiful people who then produced me. My father started work in the sugar factory, then came here to work in factories and my mother was a housewife.'
SunSum:	'Your mother was a housewife girl? Is how she lucky so?'

Chorus of laughter then chatter which creates a buzzing in the room.

Sankofa:	(Standing.) 'Alright ladies, let's keep going ... SunSum!'
SunSum:	'Sorry people, my fault ... a little tinsy bit a envy ketch mi. How I would love to be a housewife! (Laughs.) I better behave, you see how Mama B looking at me. Okay, I honour my hard-working parents from Jamaica who came here and helped the Midlands industries through factory labour. Amen.'
Akoben:	'Sankofa, I must say, I've never done anything like this before ... I like it ... it feels so right ... thanks for introducing this cultural idea to us. Okay ... Jamaica, island in the sun, you produced my father and my mum. Daddy worked in factory but was a builder too ... and mummy, there was nuttun in the kitchen that she couldn't do. RIP, mummy. Give t'anks.'
GyeNyame:	'Waxing lyrical sister, Akoben. Love it! ... Okay, this one is tricky, because I know that both my parents were from JA, but I don't know my dad. Anyway, my mum was a hard working higgler, she's who I learned my work ethics from.'
Dame-Dame:	'Higglering was hard work mi girl ... those "before day" starts with the heavy baskets on yo' head ... nuff respect to yo' mama girl. Anyway, my turn, Jamaica is my motherland, my mum worked in a Midlands chocolate factory while my father was a shoemaker. RIP both.'
Sankofa:	'Thanks all. Parts of our Caribbean culture is somewhat inseparably interwoven in the British culture which is so fast paced. It's good to just take time to acknowledge our parents ... as we say in Jamaica ... teckin' time ain't laziness.'
GyeNyame:	'Sankofa, so what about Mama B, she drop from sky or is the stork bring her?'

The room again erupts with laughter.

Sankofa:	'Thank you, GyeNyame! Sorry, Mama B, go ahead.'
Mama B:	'I honour my father's Ghanaian ancestry and in the same breath, I acknowledge the Irish roots of the maternal side of me. I represent the dichotomy between the enslaved and the slave owner, which is

very much a part of most of our realities. For our ancestral roots, mother earth, and father God, we give thanks.'

(Lifts a chicken drumstick to her mouth.) 'I have to ask this, Akoben, did you cook this jerk chicken? Your mother's skills have been inherited girl ... very tasty, very, very tasty, seems like your marinade seeped right through the bones of this drumstick.'

GyeNyame: 'Sweet fi true.'
Nsaa: 'Yeah man ... gal you can cook.'
Akoben: (Fist to her chest, taking a deep breath, then exhaling slowly.) 'So pleased you're enjoying it ... I keep mummy alive through her recipes.'
Sankofa: (Stands and walks to the centre of the circle.) 'Thanks ladies, we're going to move on. Have a refill if you want, then we are going to have our first conversation about our lived experiences of higher education. These are story sharing and sense making sessions. Each time we meet, we will be looking at differing aspects of our educational journeys. We are going to challenge each other to think for ourselves, to speak from the heart, to try to make sense for ourselves. We want to move away from the banality of labelling and accepting, to the complexities of questioning and critically analysing.'

(Pauses reflectively.)

'I need to say, that for some of us this journey will be an emotional one. But this should be a safe place to expose, deal with the hurts then build resilience to move forward. We'll see. Though we want others to know of our trajectories, first and foremost we want to learn from and make sense of our own journeys!

That's one of the reasons Mama B is here. She has dedicated her life to studying people who tried to make sense of the world we live in. People called philosophers. She will be introducing us to a whole range of philosophers through reading material.

I hope that when we link the philosophical insights to our experiences we will see what aspects of our colonial mindsets and practices we need to reject and decide how we approach inequalities differently.

Mama B will be encouraging us to engage with the ideas of some who have gone before us, whether in life, academically, spiritually or emancipatory. You know what I mean? Those who are further down "liberation lane" than we are at present.'

SCENE 3

We really wanted to be nurses

Mama B: (Stands in the centre of the circle, shuffling reams of paper.) 'So to commence, we are going to throw out a wide question. How did you come to apply for university and the foundation degree or the "Band 4 course"? Who'll start?'

Bese Saka: 'Shall I? When I heard about it, I thought ... why not build up my skills and get recognised for what I do? It was an opportunity and a way to get closer to nursing. My manager though, she was like: "Oh, I don't know if the Band 4 is going to work in this department." Blah, blah, blah, she wasn't enthusiastic. She did everything to put me off. I had to phone the course organisers and ask them to tell me my rights 'cause I didn't want to miss the opportunity.'

Akoben: 'Girl, I thought it was just me, I also had to fight for my place ... to be honest, a couple of girls on my ward had done it and I was like, so wha' dis course everybody a talk 'bout and a go pan ... how come I never hear about it? So, it's like they selected who they thought ... so I asked why wasn't I offered a chance to go? I spoke to my manager an' she goes: "you have to wait two years until the others have finished." I told her I would like the opportunity too! I applied and she informed me that she had someone else in mind. Someone who had just joined the team, but the person was off sick, so I said to the manager, "I'm here, what's the problem?" She said, "Akoben, I don't feel I need to discuss this with you if you are going to take that attitude with me." Because mi a tell yo' de truth ... mi neva nice ... So, I went over her head and then she completed the paperwork very reluctantly, really reluctantly, that's how I got my place.'

Nsoromma: 'Listening to you two, I feel fortunate, because the ward sister pushed me into it really. 'Cos I was confident at doing things on the ward, she thought I would be good at it.'

Mate Masie: 'When my manager came and said: "Mate Masie, I think that this course would be good for you, I'll get the information and you should apply". I was chuffed, I thought, oh good, someone is interested in me ... then I just wanted to big up myself, do something better, you know? And earn more money as well ...'

(Interruptions: kissing of teeth and the mumbles of 'damn lies' and other undecipherable mutters.)

Sankofa: (Stands for a few moments then leaves the room allowing space for the women to exhale. She knows the issue of not getting the promised pay rise was a very sensitive subject for those who had successfully completed the fd. After a few minutes re-enters the room.)
'Okay, ladies, can we continue, please?'

Mate Masie: 'I guess I touch a RAW nerve, but as I was saying. I also wanted to be a role model for my kids, even though they've got kids of their own now.'

SunSum: 'Like you, MM, my manager came and said, "I saw this course and, er, I think you should go for it. I think you'll do well." I thought, you know what? I've got nothing to lose, so I'll have a go. I was getting brain dead in my role so I looked forward to the challenge. Some of the other seniors weren't pleased. I'll tell you something ... I do think sometimes these people think we're dumb ... I once wrote a formal letter to complain about the conduct of a colleague and when the matron got it ... she called me in, not so much to investigate my complaint ... she kept asking me, who wrote the letter? Who wrote the letter? ... I then asked her, is something wrong with it? She said, well the way the letter is written, it doesn't seem like it was written by a HCA. That's what she said to me ... that account has never left me ... it's what she didn't say that plays with my head. That letter could not have been written by someone like you. You're only a HCA. So, I thought about all that and I thought you know, these people, they don't think we are worth anything so that encouraged me as well to go on the course.'

(Her words stun the women, at first there are faint groans, then absolute silence. The silence is weighty ...)

Sankofa: (Rises from her seat and interrupts the silence.) 'How are we feeling? You are in charge here; do you want to go on?'

(Undecipherable mutters drape the room.)

Akoma: (Slumps into her seat, voice broken.) 'Sankofa, we live it. We know how they think of us, we're not fools, we know that a lot of them think we're stupid. We just never talk about it openly, not even amongst ourselves.

So, we need to do this ... we need to hear each other's experiences, including the pain, and we need to tell our own. We need to start making sense of the subordination and unfairness. It may be too late to change things for us, so maybe what we're doing here is for our children. What do you all say?'

(In hushed voices.)

Nsaa:	'Eh, eh, alright, let's gwaan ...'
SunSum:	(Nods ... No words.)
GyeNyame:	(Makes eye contact with Akoma, raises her chin and pushes it forward indicating that she should continue.)
Akoma:	'Well, in my case, I heard about the course from colleagues on the ward. I then spoke to my manager who said: "Akoma, you are a very caring person and your patients get on well with you. You work well amongst the team, you are capable of pushing yourself to get a few more qualifications." She then helped me to complete the application form. Wha' 'bout you, Nsaa?'
Nsaa:	'Sounds like you and I had a similar experience, colleagues had done it and I was questioning myself, "oh gosh, university, oh gosh, can I do this?" Then I said, I'm gonna do it, of course I can. Yes, I can! I sound like a member of Barack Obama's 2008 campaign team, don't I?'

Some chuckle. The women welcome the distraction and chatter about President and First Lady Obama. They chatter for a few minutes.

Sankofa:	(Rises to her feet.) 'Sorry to have to break this up ladies. God knows we needed the light conversation, but can we keep going? Nsaa!'
Nsaa:	'Well, I had almost finished really, like Akoma, my manager was supportive too ... she said: "go for it ... I think you should do your nursing, but this is a first stage ... go for it."'
Aya:	(Shuffles uncomfortably in her seat.) 'I think I need to go next, as my experience mirrors that. My manager encouraged me to do nursing but the time wasn't right; neither could I afford to. She raised it again and again over the years then she said: "okay, I'm going to register you on the Band 4 course ... you go Aya and I will help you ... I will be your mentor."'

Dame-Dame:	(Trying to avoid spilling her drink, looks up awkwardly.) 'How I got on was quite straightforward really, my colleagues, seniors and patients would ask … why don't you do your nurse training? So, when I saw the fd advertised and I heard it could lead to nursing, I applied.'
GyeNyame:	(Rising to her feet and looking over at Mama B.) 'Last but by no means least, eh … if Nsaa is a member of the President Obama crew, then I'm with Dr Martin Luther King … I had a dream …'
SunSum:	(Trying hard to stifle her laughter.) 'Preach it, sister.'
Bese Saka:	(Laughing hard.) 'Amen and praise the Lord.'

The laughter is contagious, the rest of the women are no longer trying to gain composure. They are laughing uncontrollably.

Sankofa:	(Stands. But she is laughing hard too. She tries to compose herself, but each time she looks at one of the women, laughter is triggered, she's gone … she flops into her seat!)
Mama B:	(Stands and without uttering a single word, within a few moments, order is seemingly resumed.)
GyeNyame:	'Well, brethren, like the wise man said … I had a dream. (Laughter tears rolling down her cheeks she's trying to avoid eye contact with Mama B. She closes her eyes to compose herself and continues … her tone changes, her voice, broken and serious.) Throughout my childhood, my ambition was always to be a nurse. I always tell myself that my education was poor so I won't be able to do it! I always wanted to go to university, but that was a dream (a smirk etched on her face), that was just wishful thinking.

So, when the Band 4 was advertised, I looked at it, but to be honest, I didn't dare dream I could. Then Sankofa asked me why don't I give it a go … she told me that for most people, going to university was not about been gifted, it was about being disciplined. So, I decided to give it a go. I went for the interviews and got through. That's how it was for me.' |
| Sankofa: | 'Thank you. So, grateful. Re-telling our accounts ain't easy, but as someone said earlier, it's necessary. Shall we have a break and then we'll hear from Mama B. Quarter of an hour enough?' |

Lazily, bodies emerge with the noise of chairs screeching along the tiled floors. The room buzzes with chatter and laughter and there's much ribbing in store for Nsaa and GyeNyame who linked themselves to influential Black orators. Instead of punch, tea, coffee and herbal tea is poured, complimented by moist Jamaican ginger cake served on napkins.

We really wanted to be nurses

Akoben walks over to the iPad, turns the speakers on ... Labi Siffre is belting out:

> The higher you build your barriers, the taller I become, the farther you take my rights away, the faster I will run. You can deny me, you can decide to turn your face away, no matter cause there's something inside so strong. I know that I can make it. And though you're doing me wrong, so wrong, thought that my pride was gone. Oh no, something inside so strong ooh ho, something inside so strong.

At the end of the song, Akoben presses replay, this time she mouths the words as she walks away.

The group re-converge. Sankofa introduces Mama B.

Mama B: 'Well, Sankofa, thanks for the invitation. I'm already enjoying the space ... though I feel the need to lay foundation as I may not meet the expectations you all have of me. Unless we lay a sturdy foundation, what we build will be vulnerable to loss like so many efforts of the past. So, do I have your permission to go a little deep in this space? We cannot really make sense without reading. Reading is a discipline and much reading is required to help us make sense. I know that for many of us, our exposure to academic reading has not been inspirational but for us to move forward we must close that chapter and be open to read and reread and then make links from what we have read to our lived experiences.

It is also useful to share reading and ideas. So much learning is achieved through sharing. So, this won't be a space where you are taught, this should be a space where we are simultaneously teachers and students.'

GyeNyame: 'Well, let me speak for myself, I need to have a positive academic experience. I'm hoping this is going to be the place for that. I have daughters who aspire to go to university. I probably could have done things differently in my time at uni but I was building on nothing. I really want to learn how we could do it differently, I'm only 45 so I don't rule out going to university again.'

(Looks around the room with all eyes on her, her nervousness is evident in her voice.)

GyeNyame: 'Ladies, are we ready? Are we ready to read, to get disciplined? To ... what do they often say? To engage in this process and to invest time?'

(The women's smiles and nods is all the permission Mama B needs to proceed.)

Mama B: (Looking directly at GyeNyame winks then clears her throat.) 'To quote Henry Wadsworth Longfellow (1807–1882), "The heights that great men reached and kept, were not attained by sudden flight. But they, whilst their companions slept, were upward toiling through the night." Now I make no apologies for being direct here. During the break, I overheard a lot, but there are two questions that I wish to address. The first has multiple parts: Why is Mama B here? Isn't she a professor? How can she understand our journey? The second: do you really think we can make a difference? Well, the second question is a weighty one and the first important to clarify if we are going to build trust and move forward.

So here I am. Am I a professor? Yes. I am a proud, Black, female professor from the island of Jamaica. Will I understand your journey? You bet I will! Sankofa said something earlier and I liked the way she phrased it, she said, Mama B, will be using the concepts of some who have gone before us, whether in life, academically, spiritually or emancipatory; those who are further down the lane of liberation than we are at present. I am one of those who is further on, on the journey' and ladies, that's all I am! Yes, I have a title. Yes, I've earned degrees and yes, yes, yes, I too have had, and am still having my struggles with hegemony and institutional structures.'

GyeNyame: 'Now, Mama B, you haffi mine yo language ... hege ... wha?'

Mama B: (Chuckles.) 'Yes, GyeNyame ... point well-made ... hegemony, meaning those in the majority or those in power, in our world, white folk. I started where most of you are, that's my reality and as we journey together you will gain insights into my own as well as other Black academics lived experiences too. However, commiseration is not necessary. We need to enlighten ourselves, then strategise to at least try to redress the power imbalances. I want to draw your attention to a thought from professor and philosopher Cornel West (1982). He said: "Human beings possess the capacity to change their conditions and themselves, but not to perfect either their conditions or themselves" (p. 17). Change commences with one small step, such as the one we are taking today. When I say, "our reality", I mean it's the reality of Black women, wherever we live as a minority.

We will describe our undertakings through this series of meetings as: intentional "Black feminist epistemology." Simply put, it means we are serious about exploring, making sense of, then sharing knowledge from, our cultural experiences. A transformative educator, Paulo Freire, would say, today we are embarking on "an epistemological relationship to reality". By that we are accepting that we have spent time "immersed uncritically" but now, we are striving for "critical engagement" of our own lived experiences. We are working from an ontological position which is not generally found in higher education Institutions. Ontology basically means, who we are, what makes us up. So in layman's terms, we will be reliving, examining and critically reflecting on our higher educational experiences, taking into consideration our ethnicity, our gender and our culture. We will ask some hard questions of ourselves.

So, Akoben, when you said, you were not nice to your manager because you were denied access to the course. I want to lovingly speak into that ... we know how easily we are stereotyped, so we need to ensure that when we challenge others who are not like us, we use approaches that will minimise them focusing on our conduct rather than the important issue we are seeking them to address. Our aim is that we will become more self-aware and strategic so that those we work amongst will better understand us, our experiences and the provisions that will enable us to work to our potential in both education and employment settings.'

GyeNyame: 'So let me see if I get this ... WE are researching OURSELVES and telling others how and what WE want them to consider about us ... well, about flaming time!'

Mama B: (Chuckles.) 'Amen to that, sis! Now we are all going to get a little philosophical. West (1982) suggests that:

> The community understands inquiry as a set of social practices geared towards achieving and warranting knowledge, a perennial process of dialogue which can question any claim but never once and for all ... the social or communal is the central philosophical category of this pragmatist conception of knowledge. (p. 21)

West argues that in knowledge seeking the crucial component is not intuition but social practice and communal norm. So, our reflection will equip us with questions for our institutions but as importantly for ourselves. Empowering ourselves is a radical step we have avoided for too long, it's time, ladies! We will proactively share in the hope that the dissemination of our stories will contribute to improving our situations, the transforming of our realities and our mindsets.

However, ladies, listen and listen to me good ... decolonising our minds and coming to a better understanding of ourselves will not come without struggle. I like the idea of us doing this for our children but the children will have their struggles; just as our parents had theirs and we are living ours. Hegemony can disprove our history. They can, as Labi Siffre just sang, deny us, and decide to turn their faces away. When we speak from our lived experiences in the present ... the denial gets harder, not impossible, just harder!

We can use the experience of Yancey (1998) to help us as we anticipate their probable responses. Yancey suggests that the hegemonic response could include the following denials: "1. our suggestion of oppression is inaccurate or inappropriate 2. our oppressors are not the cause 3. our oppressors will select a method of correction which will fall short of correcting the structural oppressions" (p.10). Let's bear these in mind as probable critiques for destabilising the oppressors. This work will centralise us. We will be honest about what we need to do, as well as send out challenges to the institutions. Nothing about gaining equality is easy. Let's also remember that! Yancey (1998) also reminds us that: "the institutions do not see oppressions in their structures because they are not looking at it from the angle of analysis that would reveal such things as oppression" (p. 10).'

Nsaa: (Raises her hand and waits for acknowledgement.)
Mama B: 'Nsaa, please share what's on your mind.'
Nsaa: 'Based on what you've just said, I wonder if our generation are experiencing denial 3. Studies show that for decades in this country Black children have been denied educational experiences equitable to their white counterparts. We also know that professions such as nursing have been unjust in the way they placed Black and Irish women on subordinate programmes. We know that previously universities were inaccessible to people like us. But then some political party thought up widening participation. This was meant to address, or as you said in your quote, correct the structural oppression. In many cases, WP failed, I'm guessing that institutions undertaking research will be saying, they provided us with opportunities, because that's what policies do right? But what institutional research will show is, we've failed, not that the structures in place failed us!'
Mama B: (Smiles.) 'I like the connection you made there sis. I encourage you to take your thoughts another step and ask: "who should provide the counter argument?"'
Akoma: 'Well, if you ask me, that's an easy one to answer. It should be people like you Mama B. Black professors and you academics. Shouldn't

We really wanted to be nurses

it? You know the language of the institutions. In fact, you are part of the institution.'

Mama B: 'Well, here are some of my realities that may surprise you, sisters. Though I'm in the academy and I hold the titles recognised by the academy, I am not perceived to be equal to my peers in the academy. The same structures that oppress you and I as students are very much the same structures that oppress me now as a Black academic. There are an awful lot of Black and white academics who advocate for "true equality" who just get silenced. If you want to know about professional isolation, come talk with me later. In my experience, the ways my peers try to subjugate and ostracise me generally follow this sequence: implication, accusation, subordination then distanciation.

In fact, I'm currently in a season where colleagues imply my diary is not a true reflection of my commitments: their accusations spiraled within our team and I was then called by my manager who told me that the team had complained that I am not a team player, neither was I pulling my weight. The team did everything they could to exclude me from "team knowledge".

The final nail in my coffin was when cost improvement and service redesign proposals were put in place. The team had to come up with a plan, I was not invited to the meetings as they were scheduled at times I was lecturing. I heard of the final planning meeting and though I wasn't invited, I attended. My colleagues were shocked when I entered the room. I announced that I was unable to stay the duration but I would forward my suggestions to the lead person. I then looked at the team's revised organisational chart. My position alone was relegated with the recommendation that my salary be protected for two years. Subsequently, I had to spend time evidencing what I do, which was useful as it transpired I was doing more and higher quality work than my peers. To conclude, I kept my job, but who the hell can I now trust in that team? How do we move forward? 'Cause, I tell you what, when the process was over, it was back to normal FOR THEM! No one acknowledged what they had done to me. No one talked about it. It was as though nothing had happened. BUT NOT FOR ME!'

Akoben: 'Hang on a minute! Are you for real? Are you expecting us to believe that at your level you have to put up with the same shit, beg yo' pardon, as us? So why the hell do you bother getting all them degrees and titles then? I thought "you lot" up there in the ivory towers with "them" would be exempt from all that crap!'

Mama B: (Laughs, then grunts.) 'West (1998) argues that institutional oppression is covert and often denied by those within the upper echelons of the institution. I found out recently there are only eighteen minority female professors in the UK. Trust is a huge issue for them working alongside colleagues within structures. I use distanciation to protect myself. What I mean is I go to work, to work. I refuse to socialise with colleagues. Piper (1998), an African-American female Academic and Philosopher described what I do as an, "instinctual removal of ... self from the toxic contexts". I am generally an easy target because I refuse to keep my mouth shut on issues of ethics, transparency and equality. I talk to other Black men and women in the academy both here in the UK and abroad and most of them are living through some seriously weighty injustices too.

That's simply our reality! We are not, as you say, in ivory towers. Would you believe that currently, in the academy, work on the issue of race inequalities is still not seen as "real research" (Alexander 2016).

But if we are to truly engage ladies we first and foremost engage with self, how did West (1998) put it? He said:

> There is a certain kind of openness about one's own self such that people can see that you're being self-critical and they can see how you are complicitous with some of the very things you talk about. In other words, it's not simply pointing fingers or calling names, but really showing that you are in the very mess that you are trying to grasp. (p. 37)

End of quote. So, ladies, it is our hope that: "If we're willing to take a risk here and become vulnerable, then those in the institutions will open up, take a risk and become vulnerable with regard to listening to what we are saying" (West 1998: 37). But if the truth be known, the struggle certainly doesn't get easier because one has greater academic credentials or exposure.

I like to use quotes to start stories so I'll share with you a quote from Yancy (1998) who uses the words of Robert Birt, an African American philosopher. Birt wrote:

> Philosophy is often regarded as amongst the highest of human intellectual activities and manifestations of human intellectual excellence, a superior endeavour suited for "superior"

(i.e. "white") minds – hardly an endeavour for which Blacks are deemed capable or which would fit them for their 'natural' function as useful labourers. To this day, a Black philosopher is commonly regarded as a contradiction in terms, an anomaly or an undesired intruder into a realm that does not concern him or her. (p. 5)

My question is: when will Birt's "to this day" fail to be true for us Black academics or Blacks in general?'

Sankofa: (Coughs, smiles and nods.)

Mama B: (A little embarrassed looks over at Sankofa.) 'I'm sorry, ladies, I'm now doing the very thing that Sankofa and I said we were not going to do. That's ... talk too much! That cough was my cue to wrap this up and get you talking. So, in closing, we will strive to develop and share our own epistemologies. We accept we have biases and we enter this space acknowledging that our biases are based on our multiple experiences in the differing contexts.

We tend to have: "a deep suspicion of 'university philosophy or 'academic philosophy' that tends to be concerned with abstract concepts and forms of universalising and always in track of necessity as opposed to the concrete, the particular, the existential, the suffering beings we are and can be" (West, 1998: 33).

We acknowledge right from the start that our major intention here is to have our stories told, whilst also having the courage to be our self, the courage to wrestle with the truths about ourselves the truth about the NHS and the university and the courage to commence a differing kind of dialogue in our fight for justice. We know that the foundation degree programme was rolled out to: males, Asians, Whites and other mixed and or minority groups. We also know that in those groups there were "failures" too. However, here in this space, we are only interested in the journeys of Black British and Black Caribbean women.

Yancy (1998) terms what we will be engaged in here as, "dialectical conversations". He suggests such conversations are, "complex sociolinguistic interactions that function as a site of fecundity, richness, opens, tension and contestation" (p. 7). In other words, we can produce rich, new insights through our sharing together. We are engaging in "dialectical conversations" because as a group we are connected and can share our realities. Our purpose here is not to merely talk, but to make sense. To "revalidate and reconstruct" our norms in light of our lived experiences and perspectives as

Black women. We will strive to accomplish this without "universally demonising whiteness." As we dialogue we will strive to carve out some sense of intent for approaching our futures. Freire (1987) believed that education should transform lives, he suggests that "dialogue is itself creative and re-creative" so what we are doing here amounts to a form of recreating ourselves through dialogue.

So, let us recap some of the points and questions that arose from your responses to the first question in this series. Getting on to the course seemed to result from a combination of self and managers' referrals. Some of you are aspiring nurses. A couple of you fought to get on the course. What I didn't hear was: 1. How many of you researched the course yourselves prior to accepting a place? And 2. Did any of you choose your place of study? How about we look at those two questions for starters?'

The two questions Mama B posed fell straight to the tiled floor and so did the eyes of most of the women. The silence was palpable, but Mama B was not perturbed, she waited for what seemed liked minutes then she spoke again.

Mama B: 'Okay then, why did you not research the course for yourselves ladies?'

Nsaa: 'Well, Mama B, I'll start. Where I work, it's the managers who seek out our development, we have never been encouraged to do it ourselves, and to be fair, she does a good job at it, so we leave her to get on with it. If I'm honest though, I was so chuffed at the idea of going to university, I'm not sure I would have cared where I went. It was only after my daughter started researching her university place that I came to understand that universities also had league tables. Mama B, without making excuses, 'cause that was a hard-hitting question, we are the first generation to inhabit the university space, right? We are also what the institutions label "non-traditional" so who do we learn the rules of engagement from? We had no role models!'

Mama B: 'Now hear me sisters, my intention was not to criticise but to encourage us to think critically. You've raised good points there, Nsaa. It seems, your daughter has already had a more informed approach to selecting her place of study. So that's progress! So, we reflect, ask the critical questions to move forward, right? I mean ...'

Akoben: 'Mama B, can I interrupt here? All I can say is, when you've been working at a place for over twenty years with very little training

We really wanted to be nurses

and you get offered the chance to go to university, you take it. I wouldn't have dreamt of interrogating it. I just took it. But I learnt the hard way about choices, didn't I? Bloody hell, ladies, we were brought up on the saying that, nobaddy no gi yo' nuttun fi free. You know, I for one really had no excuse not to 'check out' the course. I remember Sankofa got us discussing the Tuskegee experiment in one of our Literacy classes, way back when. That was my first ever classroom lesson on thinking critically. They injected the people they had made illiterate through denying them education with a virus then fed them sweets and watched them die like a lab experiment. Nothing is free ... and certainly not for oppressed people ...'

Mate Masie: 'Hang on there, Akoben, let me say something. I remember that Tuskegee session as well, but many of us want to be nurses and we saw this as our foot in the door. But now you've asked the question, I wonder if we were just told what we wanted to hear, because our history shows we would not explore education provision for ourselves. SunSum told me that her manager thought the NHS was bringing back the SEN position. For many qualified nurses the Band 4 role was a threat, but for us, we heard: university, Band 4 and our own caseloads and that equaled professional respect, and one step closer to being a nurse. Who wouldn't jump at that opportunity? But, apart from getting into university everything else was an empty promise. My father used to tell us: "an empty promise is a comfort to a fool". That's about right, I do think the institutions see us as fools.'

Mama B: 'We must know our history, this must be amongst our principal pursuits. Black women and nursing pedagogy have historically been problematic, so the omission of knowledge of our history as well as a lack of exploration of so-called opportunities has proven to be physically, psychologically, professionally and emotionally costly. I have sourced some reading for us to explore as part of our reflection on our journeys. History hasn't done too well at teaching us about the Jamaican nurses who were pioneers of seeking an equitable nursing education during colonial times.

Ladies, ladies, knowledge not only informs, it places us in positions to liberate ourselves. So please, please read! What we are striving to do is take our experiences from the peripheries of the academic and workplace contexts and make them the centrepiece of the discussion. Sankofa, why don't you distribute the readings for the next session and explain how it will work. We are never going to have time to address everything in full, but please bring

	your reflections to the next session. Thank you, I enjoyed being with you today.'
Sankofa:	'So ladies, next week we are going to explore institutional structures and power. Some of the language in the papers I'm handing out here may be a little highbrow but, we've chosen philosophers and papers which are: not too dense, which speak about struggle and many of the philosophers are Black too. So please, let's stick with it. We will be co-facilitators of the sessions and Mama B will be here to support us. Has everyone got the next date in your diaries?'

The women stand dispersing to different parts of the room. Some gathering utensils from the kitchen, others packing up chairs, whilst GyeNyame disseminates the papers.

SCENE 4

Getting to grips with power

It's a wintery February evening in 2013. The women meet in a local church hall in Hockley, Birmingham. For sustenance, it is 'bring and share'. Akoben's responsible for the hot meats and she continues to showcase her momma's recipes. Some brought hard dough bread, whilst others brought paper plates, cups and drinks. No one dared to bring alcoholic drinks into the 'house of God'. Mate Masie unveiled her Jamaican fruit cake, preserved since Christmas. As she opens the box those nearby are hit with the aromas of rum and Red Label wine.

GyeNyame:	'Wow, Mate, girl, I guess your message is, you don't need alcohol in a bottle to enjoy it. Is how much alcohol yo' put in dat?'
Mate Masie:	(Walks away making a cross as though in confession.) 'Not a lot, an' I wouldn't lie to you, 'cause I in the house of the Lord.'
GyeNyame:	(Giving Mate Masie that 'pull the other one' look.) 'Well you know what they say, the proof of the pudding is in the eating, so if it tastes as good as it smells, save one big slice for me.'

The women serve themselves food and take their seats with food on laps and drinks at their feet as was their custom.

Pre-session chatter

Sankofa:	'Mama B I have been living with a quote from Angela Davis (1998), she said: "I never saw philosophy as separate from a social critique or from social activism" (p. 21). I have been deliberating on that quote since we last met. Davis' quote helps me in affirming my approach to this study. For me, part of my social activism is to ensure that I write up our accounts in a way that it is accessible to Black women. Our challenge however, is to keep the unity ... Davis' account also

	gave a warning not to think we are unified based just on coalition, she suggests that would be naïve, rather, we need, "a unity produced politically, around issues and political projects" (pp. 24–25).
	SunSum has been contemplating too, I think she's been reading Janice Collins' (2015) work on Active Centralised Empowerment (ACE). For today's session, she's suggested that we speak from the centre. She explained her idea to the group and the others liked it. We will keep the large circle layout but place a couple of chairs in the middle of the circle, then, whoever is going to voice her thoughts sits in the middle. I asked her why more than one chair, she said that sometimes they may wish to share in isolation whilst at other times with another who was equally passionate about the issue.'
Mama B:	(Reflectively.) 'Coalition is a good place to start Sankofa, then grow from there ... Regarding the centralising approach, love it! Let's do it! We do have a responsibility Sankofa to remind ourselves that centralising requires intentional preparation and an openness to be constructively challenged. Those interventions may be painful but questioning could also lead to decolonising the mind. We must be aware that deconstruction is often uncomfortable, and sharing our thoughts can be costly.'
Sankofa:	'I hear you, ma'am!'

Mama B stands and claps her hands to gain the attention of the women. The chatter eventually ceases and plates are stored underneath chairs.

Mama B:	'Welcome to session 2, ladies. I'm pleased we all made it through the icy temperatures to be here. Thanks for the delicious soul food and positive energies you've already started to generate. You women are amazing! I'm learning so much ... I'm loving what Freire calls "reciprocal learning". On the board, she writes the following quote:

> So long as the determination of a person's income is not only *beyond democratic control and public knowledge, but is a matter of autocratic power and secret manipulation*, just so long the application of logic and ethics to wealth, industry and income is going to be a difficult if not insoluble problem. (W. E. B. DuBois, 1973: 101)'

'Now there is a meaty quote, in pairs, read it, re-read it, discuss for a few minutes then as you talk, if any part of this quote resonates

Getting to grips with power 35

                  with you, make the link as you share. I'll give you five minutes then we'll start sharing.'

GyeNyame: 'I would like to talk about how the two institutions (the university and the NHS Trust) we work and study in has power to influence and secretly manipulate rendering us as "failures". They offer us "opportunities" though from time and memorial, as my grandma would say, their autocratic power over us was to control us by determining our fixed status and income. No Band 4 for you ... we have satisfied the funders, placed you on the course and will use your skills if you quality but ... man, this is tough! Anyway ... I read a couple of the articles you gave us. I'm not saying that I fully understand, it was like being back at uni again. (She giggles somewhat awkwardly.) But I think I understand or, should I say, I'm accepting that this journey is going to be painful. How can confronting deception and exploitation be anything but ... both at work and at uni as a Black woman, I feel completely powerless! I'm not sure if this is what you wanted when you talked about us making a link Ma B ...' (Looking directly at her for a response.)

Mama B: 'Well, power is a topic of breadth and depth so you just make a link to any aspect of the quote when you feel it resonates. Just whilst you've stopped for the moment, GyeNyame, I think SunSum has shared the idea of centralising the speaker, so are you ready to take the centre seat as you carry on sharing?'

GyeNyame: 'No, not really, will someone join me please? Akoben?'

Akoben: 'I really don't trust myself when thinking about power dynamics, much more talking about it, but this should be a safe space, so I'll join you.'

GyeNyame: 'Thanks, sis. I must say Mama B's questions at the end of the last session hit me hard. Real hard! I couldn't help feeling that I had allowed myself to be "used" for someone else's gain or agenda. The more I thought about it and shared it with my husband, the sicker I felt. Now, I'm not about to heap guilt on myself, for me, this is more about learning and I have learnt that a lack of exploration contributed to my exploitation. I spoke to my daughters about their university application processes and it was then that I fully understood the magnitude of the question. To be honest, I was not involved in my daughters' university application processes. The sixth form tutor did it all. Another lesson there for me!

So, here are a couple of things that haunted me since the first session: 1) we had no choice about where or what we studied. 2) I hadn't really researched the course. We went to a university chosen by our workplace and though some of us knew others who had finished the course before we started, we didn't check whether on completion they had been appointed to the new roles they were promised. As I reflected I thought, lack of research exposed us to some inequitable and poor practices and ultimately to exploitation and disappointment. To try and emphasise this, let me throw out a question. How was your induction? I'm hoping that we can attempt to ... make a link to power here, Mama B.'

Mama B: 'Okay, go for it.'

Nsoromma: 'Well, that's easy for me. Three little words ... didn't have one!'

Bese Saka: 'Seriously, Nsoromma? We had two, the induction at work was fun actually. I did a presentation, I was a bit nervous but it was alright. Uni induction was a bit chaotic. You know, you had to get your ID, you know, the big panic and you felt a bit ... out of it really.'

Mate Masie: 'I don't know if what I had was an induction. I'll tell you this. I remember this woman coming to talk to us, she made the course sound very interesting, after her talk I felt good, couldn't wait to go ... (Laughing.) You know, I felt good, I just felt excited ...'

Nsaa: 'I felt really good about going to uni on day one. I was looking forward to being with others of like mind and gaining knowledge of the campus and services. Instead ... I walked into the room, a large lecture theatre, looked around the room and thought ... where's the Black people? (Laughing.) I did. But for me, it was that feeling that I'm here in university and I feel good. I felt important and thought ... I'm here, but where are the others like me? Didn't have a proper induction though.'

Dame-Dame: 'Like Bese Saka, my first work-based meeting was made fun. You got to meet one or two of the tutors from the university. They came to the workplace to talk to us with one of the former students. The student gave us an insight on what to expect. But as we went through the course ourselves, we realised that what the student gave us was the sanitised marketing version. I didn't have a university induction.'

SunSum: 'Induction, naah, it was so quick. Erm, it was on the Trust site. They told us the modules, what we would be doing, but it was all ... it just went pass me really. I didn't really understand the depth of it. We didn't have a uni one either, the tutors came into the workplace and that was where we had our so-called induction.'

Akoma: 'You know something; my induction was quite strange actually. They did icebreakers and stuff, but err, really, erm, I don't think they can quite prepare you for what happens throughout your stay.'

Getting to grips with power 37

Akoben: 'So we're the centralised ones. Now let me get this right, SunSum. Those on the outside of the circle represent women in society in general. Those of us in the middle are symbolic of bringing the issues of Black women from the outside, where we live it, but never talk openly about it. Taking this position means we have something to say and our voices won't remain hidden or silenced. We need to speak out to academics, our colleagues, our workplaces and maybe even our societies. But am I right in thinking that we are also talking to ourselves ... yeah? Well, I'm going to be blunt. From the start, I felt ... uni ... you know what ... it's just a big wide world and nobody gives a shit about ya! I tell you the ... that's how I felt when I started ... I tell you the truth ... when I started uni ... everybody else seemed to know what they were doing ... I didn't. They were getting it ... I was like ... shit ... so what am I supposed to do? What am I supposed to be doing?' In my case, there wasn't much guidance at first you know. This reliving thing brings back the confusion and hurts man ... teck over GyeNyame please ... I need to gather my thoughts.'

GyeNyame: 'Everyone is looking at me. You see, I've already learned a lesson just listening to you all. What if we had talked to each other? We would have known that most of us felt like fishes out of water. But we never shared that, did we? Because we never shared, we all ended up finding our way to Despondency Street in isolation. If only we had shared ... Well ... my induction, to be honest it was quite scary. I was scared because we didn't know what to expect. It was our first day and I remember when the lecturers talked, everything they told us, they teck up a book. (Laughing quite loudly.) I never figet this one woman it's like ... she was talking about academic writing and plagiarism – she teck up a book. Stella Coxwell, was a name of one of the authors. I remember the tutor used Coxwell's name for almost everything.

But no joke, everything they said they mentioned a book. I think, I left with the names of between ten to twelve books. I say, I left with the names, but I didn't. The lecturers talked so fast Coxwell was the only one I got down. I went to my induction in the dark and I left in the dark. What more can I say? Does anyone want to add anything?'

(The room is silent, so she continues.)

GyeNyame: 'The NHS and Universities are well-established institutions with clear standard operating policies. What does our induction experiences tell us about power? Ball (2008) suggests that, "the concept of knowledge economy was introduced by Drucker in 1966, where he made clear distinctions between the manual worker and the so-called knowledge worker" (p. 19). That word "economy" kept cropping up in the papers I read. Ball (2008) goes on to say that:

> within policy, education is regarded primarily from an economic point of view. The social and economic purposes of education have collapsed into a single, overriding emphasis of policymaking for economic competitiveness and an increasing neglect or sidelining of the social purposes of education. (pp. 11–12)

End of quote. I was invited onto the Band 4 programme and I'll be honest, the promised wage rise was as important to me as the anticipated university experience. I now understand that the introduction of the opportunity to attend university was an economic endeavour. The institutions got me, they lured me into their web where they could exploit my skills, as they had done with my parents' generation. And what was their bait? Economic uplift! ... Shit ... I guess they always knew the uplift was never going to happen. I laughed when my husband pointed out that the government got done too, as our courses were government funded. But as a tax payer, I guess it means it wasn't the government, it was all of us working people. As we strive to make sense of the links between us being offered the foundation degree and the state of our economy, let's hear the words of Tony Blair, our former Prime Minister. Akoben, have you got that section with the quote?'

Akoben: 'Yes, I think this is the bit you want me to read. Blair (2005) states that:

> The purpose of the reforms is to create a modern education system and a modern NHS where at last the levels of investment are coming up to the average of our competitors, real power is put in the hands of those who use the service, the patient and the parent where the changes are becoming self-sustaining, the system open, diverse, flexible able to adjust and adapt to the changing world. (p. 15)

Is that where you wanted me to stop?'

GyeNyame: 'Thanks, Akoben, ladies, did we get that? We were to be given real power! How in the world were we given any power at all much less

Getting to grips with power

	real power, when right at the entry point, they "failed" us? How important should a comprehensive induction have been to first generation, mature, day release, employed students? I mean ...'
Akoben:	'GyeNyame, I see the link you're making, but I wonder if it would help if we defined induction. What is an induction? I looked it up. The Oxford dictionary states that an induction is: "the action or process of introducing someone to an organisation or establishing them in a position." Sorry, but I feel the need to repeat that – for emphasis. An induction is: "the action or process of introducing someone to an organisation or establishing them in a position." So, we were placed in a higher education institution without been given the knowledge of how to be established in it. Set up to fail, right from the start! GyeNyame's right! Now I've started, I just want to get a few things off my chest. I read Freire (1987), he said, and I quote:

> if we are able to make readers uneasy, fill them with some uncertainty, then what we do will be important, if we achieve that, our work will be rigorous. (p. 4)

	I'm no academic but I want us to attempt to show rigour in our work so we are not dismissed as a group of storytellers. When our readers engage, our accounts should create responses on many levels. I know we are only a small group of women in non-powerful roles, but we can work to high standards, can't we ... ?'
Mama B:	'You're right, Akoben, but I think it was the same Freire (1987) who said that: "what is rigorous today may not be tomorrow as rigour is not universal" (p. 4). Freire thought differently about pedagogy, another word for teaching, so he's really giving us license, if ever we needed it, to go ahead with thinking differently and ...'
Sankofa:	'Yes, and from my experience, doing things differently can be slow, filled with anxiety and be messy too, because there's no one correct script to follow. But, it's liberating and offers so much learning ... hey, let's do it ... let's journey on a road less travelled ... what do you say?'
GyeNyame:	(Voice breaks with emotion.) 'What do you mean messy? Is there a non-messy option for people like us? Mess is what we are expected to wade through every time, it's our reality! And we are not victims, we become more resolute, knowledgeable, resilient and determined because of our wading.

Earlier, didn't you refer to a philosopher West ... hang on ... I wrote it down ...'we are in the very mess we are trying to grasp.'

(Silence overtakes the surroundings; the noiselessness is awkward. Sankofa waits to see if Mama B will interject something motivational. She doesn't ... she's busily thumbing through a book ... it seems like minutes pass ... then Nsaa speaks.)

Nsaa: 'Akoben, may I take the centre for a moment please? My reading was Freire and Pedagogy and there are a couple of links that I can try to make with power also. I would like to further explore power and the lack of proper induction. I want to use a few quotes here ... Freire (1987) states – it's a long quote, but please bear with me:

Education does not shape society ... it is society which shapes education according to the interests of those who have power. If this is true, we cannot expect education to be the lever for the transformation of those who have power and are in power. It would be tremendously naive to ask the ruling class in power to put into practice a kind of education which can work against it. If education was left alone to develop without political supervision, it would create no end of problems for those in power. (p. 36)

End of quote.
He went on to say that 'transformation' can only be accomplished by those who 'dream' about the reinvention of society. Hey, there's something to be said for us dreamers. In this space, we are dreaming that we can probably shine light into how institutions, as GyeNyame said, accept us in darkness and uses power dynamics that ensure we exit in darkness or remain in professional obscurity in our workplaces. Universities are large complex sites, so for part-time students not to have an induction is a travesty of equality ... The AP role was new, all our colleagues on our wards should have been inducted into how to integrate this new role too ... I'll swap places again, Akoben.'

Akoben: 'Wow ... well said, Nsaa ... those in power would not really want us to be given the knowledge to be established in the institution as, I don't know, it may "threaten" their power? Several qualified nurses thought that the Band 4 role would be a threat! If we have no power, we are no threat, are we? Anyway, are we done for now, GyeNyame?'

Getting to grips with power

GyeNyame: 'Yeah, let's give others a chance. Being central is okay actually ladies, come on have a go.'

Akoben: 'Mama B, Sankofa, I think we're done for now.'

(GyeNyame and Akoben return to their seats on the peripheries.)

Mama B: (Rises and takes the centre seat.) 'Thanks all. There's so much there in what you've said that linked to Dubois' opening quote, you have started to think about power and structural manipulation, maybe these are themes that we will return to in future sessions. For now, however, I'd like to pick up on a couple of points. Nsaa walked into university and asked herself, "where are the Black people?" That's an important question, because for most of us, our social worlds have a very strong Black presence. Supplementary school teachers, colleagues, some of us even attend predominantly Black places of worship so it can be perplexing to find ourselves in a context where we are the only Black person. I do wonder how often whites and particularly bourgeoisie, I mean, middle-class whites, have such an experience.

It may be worth saying here that David, et al. (2010) undertook studies on widening participation in higher education and found Nsaa's experience represented amongst other Black, Minority Ethnic (BME) students. They found that some BME students chose universities because they had a representation of BME students. You, however had no choice about where you studied. The lack of choice was also an issue, you were denied the social mobility that higher education offers to so many of its students. Hold that thought!

Then again, the pain was palpable as we talked about the messiness of life's struggles and sense making. Let's consistently recall the message from West (1998) that I quoted earlier and that GyeNyame also referenced. We should expect our journeying to be somewhat messy, and messiness is okay. So, ladies, as we become vulnerable in this space, sometimes "starting with the woman in the mirror, asking her to consider and maybe change her ways" then others are inspired or challenged to make themselves vulnerable. Those "othered" folk who have a similar mindset may also be challenged to give us an audience and create spaces for us to co create dialogue. But, we must accept that within the Black communities there are power and gender struggles that must also be navigated and, it could be argued, our internal power struggles contribute to experiential mess.

Thank you, ladies, I'm sure that we will return to power as we journey in our meetings, it's amazing how time flies, we have not even scratched the surface!

Remember the next meet up will be our visit to the NHS England's conference where Sankofa will be in dialogue with a member of the national commissioning team. The dialogue is one session of their conference on Widening Participation. I wonder if we could meet say, 12:30 for a huddle. We will discuss the dialogue in session 3. God bless and safe journeys home.'

SCENE 5

Did anyone think this through?

NHS England's Conference – 27 July 2013 – The Drum, Birmingham

(12:45. The women meet Sankofa for a quick huddle.)

    Sankofa: 'Thanks for coming, ladies, I really do appreciate you all. Mmara has been quite prescriptive about what I can and can't ask, but I've got your points for exploration and I'll try to get in as many as I'm able to. More importantly, I will try to get information that can assist us in making sense. Wish me luck!'

(Women voicing encouragement and affirmation.)

    GyeNyame: 'Quickly everyone, I would like to suggest that at the next session we look at our experiences of "getting through". We agreed that we would go ahead though only half the group will be present. I would also like to suggest that the next session is held in a home ... what do you think? If you are willing, I could open my home for it. Is that okay?'
    Bese Saka: 'I won't be there, but I'll send my thoughts.'
    Nsoromma: 'Me too.'
    Sankofa: 'Sounds like a good idea GyeNyame but I think you should run it by the others and see how they feel too. I know you don't do emails much but it may be a quick way to get the views of everyone.'

(The women disperse to find seats.)
    (1:10. The interview commences – Sankofa is interviewing Mmara-Krado from NHS England's commissioning team.)

    Sankofa: 'Thanks for having me, I'm looking forward to today's dialogue. I would also like to welcome my colleagues who have an interest in this section of your conference. Mmara, could you commence by telling us how the role of the Assistant Practitioner came about?'

Mmara:	'Welcome ... okay, well, APs emerged within the last three or four years, and it is a methodology to bridge healthcare and the workforce shortfall. We know from national intelligence that we have an ageing NHS workforce population. Within the next five years we are going to see many people leaving the health service, those who are nursing which is the biggest cohort of healthcare professionals in the NHS ... the ones who are in their early fifties ... because you have the right to retire at 55 and now, with how the government is playing with pensions, a lot of people are going to take the opportunity to get out just in case anything changes. So, the national workforce intelligence is telling us that there are many nurses coming up to age 55, the nursing retirement age and that there is a possibility that many of these people will take early retirement because of the economic changes. And so that will put a gap in the nursing supply.'
Sankofa:	'And yet, my observations are that many of the staff that have gone on to the fd programme have been mid to late thirties and older. Though they won't be able to afford to retire at age 55 based on their salaries, will they? So that's how they benefit the NHS.'
Mmara:	'Erm, yes, that's true and I suppose, there's a couple of other reasons for the fd selections at that age ... one, the AP role is an opportunity for those who are silent ... those who have always wanted to be a nurse and do more clinical duties this is an opportunity for them to do it. If you recall, we used to have the SEN role. There are similarities between the AP and the SEN. The SEN was a two-year training programme. The AP is a two-year training programme. The key difference is that, as an SEN you went on to NMC registration whereas an AP now can't and the other difference is about the issuing of medication.'
Sankofa:	'If I was to give an observation here, it would be that the project 2000's aim was to get rid of the tiers of nursing.'
Mmara:	'Yes, that's how come they stopped the enrolled nurse training.'
Sankofa:	'Hmm, so has it just been brought about in another guise?'
Mmara:	'Well, going back to the start of our conversation, it has been driven by the assumptions that have been made that a lot of people are going to retire and there is going to be a gap and we are not going to feed that food chain as quickly as we need to. And not only that, but I'm sure that through your economic analysis, you'll know that we are going through an unprecedented change in this country regarding the NHS where money is very, very short.

So not only have we got a picture of mass exodus of people coming up for retirement in nursing, we can't afford the workforce we need. We need a lot more people in the healthcare service than we did twenty years ago because people are living longer. So, healthcare services are under considerable demands. So, if the demand goes up, we must meet that demand with supply. And how we give those supply is through workforce, so it's those scales that we must balance. We're expecting a mass exodus whilst demands are going up with all the shortfalls in funding.

So, this role has been born out of that. The aspirations are that we would be bridging the gap. But it's hoped that this role, whilst it's not an enrolled nurse, will give some capacity to qualified practitioners with ... There is some national intelligence that suggests that there was a lot of qualified practitioners doing clinical functions or activities that could be assigned to a lower band. If you used an AP, even if you saved 10/20/30 per cent of what that registered nurse would be, it makes that product cheaper. It gives more capacity to the registered nurse to take up some of the higher-level demands and brings down the whole workforce demand for that practitioner, so it's a conundrum really, but they do feature APs in the conundrum in getting everything balanced for the future.

From a strategic planning point of view, in theory it's good. In theory, it balances the books, it brings you the head count, it makes nursing affordable, it attempts to ensure that our service users get the right treatment with the right people looking after them in the right place at the right time and all that rhetoric.

There are a lot of hurdles to jump. As you know the NHS is quite steeped in culture, it is quite hierarchical. I don't know whether I should say organisation ... but function and there is some resistance in people/clinicians working with APs. I mean, if I focus on nursing, nursing is very ... "it's my patient" and to say you are going to hand over some of your activities to somebody else for your patients makes nurses a bit nervous because 1. from the accountability point. 2. it's my patient and 3. actually having the easier tasks within your day of work, gives you that little bit of respite as well ... I know through planning as well that it's going to come up to some buffers, there will be challenges.'

Sankofa: 'Are you anticipating tensions within the profession?'

Mmara: 'There will be tensions, there will be ... I don't know whether you have looked at this bit, like how skills are worked out on a ward.

	What I mean by that is how many Band 7s, Band 6s, Band 5s, 4s, 3s, 2s and 1s. Well, the quotas are predominantly driven by professional judgement so it will be senior nurses and interested team members that will take responsibility ... a matron could have two senior nurses and one will be flying the flag for APs and the other not and it's purely based on professional judgement.'
Sankofa:	'So you're saying that the guidance isn't mandatory, I don't understand that.'
Mmara:	'Okay and whilst a Matron or manager will use everything, evidence wise to try and influence the culture, the thinking ... at the end of the day you can't overrule that professional lead for that particular area. So, whatever the personal view of the managing nurse is, that's what governs whether APs will be employed or not. You mentioned tensions, remember that some nurses wanted the SEN role abolished, so if the AP is perceived to be a back-door re-entry. The role will not be welcomed or supported.'
Sankofa:	'Oh yeah, that's quite interesting because, at the outset of the conversation you said it was driven by economics ...'
Mmara:	'But nurses don't do economics ...'
Sankofa:	'But shouldn't they?'
Mmara:	'They don't ... they don't ... they're not ... they're not ... they want to look after their patients, they don't care what it's costing. They just want to look after their patients. Their thoughts are: "you at the top sort it out!" And if they're gonna look after their patients, they want good staff on the shop floor. So initially they'll think, I don't want "no watered-down Band 5." I want a Band 5 and that's what the advocates of the AP role will be up against.'
Sankofa:	'Right, from what I've read, the fd is a national programme and some NHS hospitals have really gone for it. Manchester seems to be one area where the Band 4 role has really taken off, in fact I know someone personally from the Trust that I work in who has relocated to Manchester after completing the programme with us and not being able to secure a Band 4 role. So nationally ... I don't know is it ...'
Mmara:	'I'm quite surprised you said that because nationally there are discussions on safer staffing models, looking at the skills mix for new hospitals and what type of workers we will need. I know your Trust has trained APs but hasn't placed most of them in AP roles. And there was ... you see, what you need to know is, were the APs counted in the qualified numbers?'
Sankofa:	'Right, well, I don't know that!'

Did anyone think this through?

Mmara: 'Okay, now whilst you refer to Manchester, it will be interesting to know how they are using APs. If they are using them to improve competence availability within the environment as opposed to using them in the trained staff numbers, then that makes sense. They're very fortunate. Okay, I bet they haven't reduced their Band 5 numbers or their Band 6 numbers. It will be interesting to see their profile from before they used the AP to now when they are using the APs. Now, sure, if you said to clinical leaders, we are going to give you Band 4s instead of Band 2s, they would say, give them to me please! We are going to include Band 4s as part of your 1–5s in your establishment but it's not going to impact on your 5, 6, and 7s very much, they'll say, give them to me. If you start saying we are going to skills mix your Band 5s across the Band 4s, taking out some Band 5 and replacing them with 4s, you've got a different argument. So, you need to understand how they are using them.'

Sankofa: 'Okay, I didn't know of all the complexity of that, so I haven't explored that, but ...'

Mmara: 'Yeah, but you have to understand that! And regarding the role of APs nationally, a lot of nurse leaders are saying no, we're not using Band 4s because what's the point? Because, at the end of the day, as you know the care set up, Band 4s will be replacing Band 5s. I think, I don't know ... a Band 4, when they get to ... I don't know ... maybe 3rd from the top on the pay scale, they'll be earning the same as a newly qualified Band 5. Then it's the same as a 2nd year Band 5, then a 3rd year Band 5 because they've moved up the pay scale. So, the manager's argument is fair enough, why would you take an AP who can't do drugs ... when they might as well take a newly qualified Band 5 who, after 6 months you know, they can be doing their own drugs? You will never be able to give a Band 4 a patient without supervision. These are some of the issues and challenges here, but what we have to define is, what we want from the AP role and how far do we want them to go?'

Sankofa: 'My question would be, was this knowledge known prior to the introduction of the Band 4 role, or is this something that's just been found out?'

Mmara: 'The way the NHS is now, the shortfalls, the concerns, the demands. Everyone should be saving money. People do "knee jerk" and don't always think things through, and I know, training has been done locally. I know that there are a number who have either left or have backed out of the course, working as they were before. Going back to your question before that, you've noticed that there are a lot of

40 plus people going into the programme, erm, yeah. I don't know if it's a good or a bad thing. It's good that people get the opportunity to realise their dreams, because you will have, maybe a significant number of Black people who have sat in HCA posts as a Band 2 and now here is an opportunity to, you know, fly. Whilst there's been a lot of mature students, erm, the attrition rates are a bit worrying. Because people are jumping to this dream but things have changed so much academically that they had to get through those academic hoops as well, it may prove different to what they think it was going to be. Okay, and we must be careful that we don't do an injustice to those aspirant HCAs. When we are gonna start looking at trends and say: "well a lot of Black people have gone on this, and they are not getting through", there needs to be critical research which informs us.'

Sankofa: 'Yeah. Well, this study will be part of the critical research you refer to. And from what I'm gauging I understand what has been said but personally, I'm quite sad that more research wasn't done up front. Because what you identified as the women falling by the way, erm, I wonder if part of them "falling by the way" was because the systems weren't rigorously researched and implemented especially around the areas of need and support.'

Mmara: 'You mean the attrition rates?'

Sankofa: 'Well, yes, if the nursing leads were resolute they were not going to use APs, then why would they invest the skills of their Band 5s and others to train and mentor the APs and why give aspiring HCAs this false hope?'

Mmara: 'If you think about what we've seen here so far, it was always gonna be difficult, for a particular group, it was going to be difficult anyway. But it was going to be more difficult for groups, if you think about, erm, ok, let's think about the fact that I said culturally, nursing doesn't particularly want APs, and what you don't want, you don't support very well. A student nurse is a traditional role, nurses understand student nurse status, they know what the product is. They will be quick to impart learning and share learning because they want that product at the end of the day. So that's number one okay. Number two, I mean, I don't know what the demographics of your APs that have gone off, if it's been 20 per cent Asian, 10 per cent Caribbean, and 50 per cent Caucasian, I don't know but if there is a number from a BME group, then they will struggle again, because you are not going to find that mentorship.'

Sankofa: 'Okay, why is that absent?'

Mmara:	'You will find mentorship, ok, and supervision, but it takes more than the given mentorship and the given supervision. You need somebody out there that will go the extra mile with you. Black women generally find it difficult to get a supervisor. A supervisor, someone they can sit with and trust. Because that's what it's about trust, some one that you can trust. I can't do this assignment here so can you give me some guidance? You must give something of yourself to build trust, friendship ... As there are so few Black managers around, for those that come from the BME communities, they are not going to find that supervision. I'm not saying that is totally the fault of it, but it ... That is going to be a difficulty, so needs thinking about.'
Sankofa:	'One of the issues I guess is that the Windrush generation of nurses didn't do the academic route into nursing and so the perception is, they are fantastic nurses, but academically, they may not be best equipped to support APs ... I don't know ...'
Mmara:	'Nursing now in the computer age is totally different, it's totally different ... it's very different. If you do have clinicians out there on the wards that don't understand how to access intelligence that can help them with their practice; that's concerning because we must move with the times. You do, so that's another subject right. But yeah, I can understand that. So, one of the areas it may be useful for your group to discuss later is: are AP students just going to Black clinicians as mentors and if so, why?'
Sankofa:	'I do question WP, the whole concept of it, if you are going to take someone in who hasn't had the luxury of going through formal education in the same way that a traditional student would have done. Then surely, that should have been part of the preparation to think, well these are non-traditional learners so we are going to have to put pastoral care in ...'
Mmara:	'And use a non-traditional approach to pedagogy ... let's be frank here, WP is a good idea, in one breath, but I don't know if it is in another. And I say that because I recall just after the Conservatives had got in and they cut down on commissions as a result we didn't have enough nurses so we did overseas recruitment and ... what they did they call it? "Widening the edge gate into nursing."
	Now what you have are programmes which were driven by the government with a cash incentive and bums on seats for HE institutions to get their income ... so, if you were to say things like, there are practitioners out there that can't or won't support the APs, that wouldn't surprise me ... Things have changed you know, since Mid

Staffs. So, if APs are saying they are not developing clinical skills and being professionally developed then the Trusts have failed ... they've failed ... this started with the Trusts. The Strategic Health Authority whips all the trusts around to get APs, whether they like it or not, get them on a course and this is what happened. And so, when people are forced, or made, to champion something that they may or may not believe in, which may or may not have been thought out thoroughly, this is the consequence.'

Sankofa: 'I look forward to the evaluation of the AP project, though we know, people can make evaluations say what they want them to say. I doubt, however, that anyone will want to say we have just thrown multiple thousands at this with very little to show for it, especially as we are supposed to be cost saving. Thanks, Mmara. That was really insightful.'

SCENE 6

If only we had known

(The doorbell rings at GyeNyame's home, she opens.)

GyeNyame: 'Hi, welcome to my humble abode. I see you've all arrived together.'
Nsaa: 'Yeah, it was Akoben's idea for us to travel together and I'm glad we did ... I'm not sure I would have found it by public transport.'
Akoben: 'Have you been baking GyeNyame? The aroma in here reminds me of bygone lazy days with the grandkids.'
GyeNyame: 'I'll take your coats, go on through to the living room and help yourselves to snacks and drinks ... don't be shy and let me know if you need anything else. I'll join you in a minute.'
Mama B: (Grabs Sankofa's arm.) 'Let's have a quick word. Sankofa, as we are in a home this evening we need to negotiate time as it can be so easy to get carried away because we are comfortable. Having said that, shall we ask the women how they want to work with the timing?'
Sankofa: 'That's true ... okay, I'll mention it.
Welcome everyone, to use the time well, shall we start, I'm sure we'll be okay to enjoy the cuisine as we share ... is that okay, GyeNyame?'
GyeNyame: 'Oh please, feel at home.'
Sankofa: 'Well, we knew that numbers-wise we were going to be a bit thin on the ground. Since the conference, I have had a couple of long telephone conversations where our sisters wanted to share their reflections following what they found out at the conference. Some felt so strongly that they took to writing and have sent me some of their experiences of "getting through". Let's remember them as we journey tonight. Bese Saka and Nsoromma were particularly affected.'
GyeNyame: 'As you all know I am a Christian, so I hope you won't mind if I open with prayer and I will also say a word for our sisters who are struggling. Some go for counselling, others to drinks and drugs ... I go for prayer.'

(She intones a prayer and at the end, everyone quietly says, Amen.)

Sankofa: 'What do you think, shall we start with the accounts the ladies sent of their experiences of "getting through" the course? Mama

SCENE 6

GyeNyame: B, could you please read Bese Saka's? Oh, before we do, I think we need to agree how we will manage the time tonight.'

Sankofa: 'I suggest we leave it fluid ... there's been a lot of unaired feelings from the conference and we need time to work through it, the group's discussed it and everyone agrees.'

Mama B: 'Okay then. So, Mama B, could you please read Bese Saka's?'
(Walks to the centre and sits on the floor.) 'Sure. So, this is Bese Saka's piece everyone.

"Hello comrades, I can't tell you how deeply the interview with Mmara affected me. It was heartrending to find out that we, and I mean all those who did the fd whatever colour or gender were just objects in the hands of strategists and policy makers. And to be honest, I use the labels 'strategists' and 'policy makers' loosely because you would think that competent 'policy makers' and 'strategists' would know what they were doing.

Though I was hurt and just wanted to 'shut down' – I didn't. For me, it now makes sense why the clinical Band 4 role evaded us. The knowledge from the conference has made me more determined to let others know what I endured on a promise that was never properly thought through and as a result, was never to be. I tell you this, ladies, the knowledge from the conference has also made me want to really invest in this project. So, listen up, Bese Saka has been reading and will be philosophising. Go on laugh, I'm not there to hear ya, but I'm serious.

Freire (1987) said:

> the more you understand the mechanisms of economic oppression and exploitation, the more you understand what working for wages really is, the more you illuminate, the more you put light on some obscurity necessary for domination. (p. 4)

We thought at the time that our Trust and our clinical leaders were 'supporting' us. Some of us may even have thought that they saw our worth and were willing to create opportunities for us to professionally develop. After all, many of them had encouraged us into nursing, but financially that option was ruled out. If we had been cynics, we would have been perceived to be ungrateful. In the current climate and with our histories in the Trust, was it wrong that we didn't even consider whether the widening participation offer was a credible one? Ladies, I laughed out loud when I read this quote from Freire (1987):

getting a job (a promised promotion in some of our cases) was a concrete and realistic expectation of HE. (p. 68)

Now I'm glad I'm writing this and not speaking it, because some of these names are, as one would say, rather challenging to pronounce. I can hear you all laughing, please pay attention, this is serious! Bourdieu, I think he's white and French, talked about 'conversion strategy.' I talked this through with Sankofa, and ladies it made sense. As healthcare assistants on pay band 2 of the NHS' hierarchical banding structure we have limited and often insufficient economic resources. Because of our economic positioning, it was impossible for us to give up our jobs and go off to university to train as nurses. We all know, because we live it, there are not enough members of clinical teams that respect the role of the HCA so we have no symbolic capital at all. Not professional anyhow.

They will often enjoy our cultural capital in the sense of our dress, food, music and social life. So, we do have this strange, complex, work, social life relationship. Stay with me ladies, I'm at the main point now, philosophising is not easy ... we hoped that the sacrifice of engaging in HE/NHS fields, seats of social capital a respected professional status would materialise for us. It was our expectation that our new professional status would lead to economic capital, the Band 4 position.

Okay, in lay man's terms, we hoped that our education would be converted into a more fulfilling role with better pay ... got it! Instead, we've come to understand that because the 'strategy' was a 'knee-jerk reaction' that we, an already subordinated group were only to reap exploitation and professional relegation for our sacrifice. Now here are some of my recollections of 'getting through' the educational experiences.

'Couple of times I felt ... why am I doing this? Shall I give up? But to be honest, my family kept me going. It wasn't the uni part that was most challenging, though some of it was. It was work. Sometimes, I would go and offload at home and my family were like: you can't give up now, you have come so far, you have struggled, you fought to be on this course. There's a reason you were meant to be doing this you know. My eldest son was like, mum, don't give up. I took courage from the family and in those tough times I said, you know what, 'the system' is not going to beat me ... I decided that I'm not giving 'them' the satisfaction of seeing me giving up because they would love that. That's what drove me. I wanted to show the people at work ... for me, passing this course means I could be a Band 4 and they didn't want to see me in that position.

When I passed the course, I made a big thing of it ... you should have seen the shock on their faces. Yeah, they were all shocked, because like SunSum said in an earlier session, they think we're dumb. My manager blatantly asked me, how did you pass, when ... a Caucasian colleague is struggling?' The very elements of my culture, which are perceived to be 'weak', our family structures, was what got me through. My cultural habitus provided me with all I needed to survive in the fields of higher education and the NHS Trust and to come out with my diploma. I'm looking forward to seeing you all when we will be talking about workplace mentoring and university support. I hope we've got a whole day for that one. Shalom ladies. Writing has helped to calm me down. I hope it all made sense."

Mama B: (Places the papers on the floor and runs her eyes around the group.)

'That's the end of Bese Saka's piece. Well, she really used her readings well. I'm pleased with her time investment, because frustration at injustice led to her being proactive.

The Jamaican born philosopher, Gordon (1998) described himself as a: "praxis intellectual" because his life is: "submerged in community organisations and the struggles of those who access them". There is a quote our parents handed down which said, "feels it, knows it" and I guess we could add, "and they should share it". To quote an African American philosopher, Harris (1998), our "philosophy is born of struggle: struggle to overcome, overcoming adversity, overcoming exclusion, overcoming a lack of 'authentic opportunity' and overcoming exploitation" (p. 219). I guess those of us in this room can say amen to that ... over to you, Sankofa.'

Sankofa: (Rises to read.) 'Whilst the room is quiet, I had a thought that I just want to throw out there. Can you see the impact we can have even in our absence? Bese Saka isn't here, yet ...'

GyeNyame
Sankofa: (Interjects.) 'Her words have impacted us powerfully.'

'Exactly! I'll now read what Nsoromma wants to share.

"Hi sisters, we were duped, weren't we? We were offered a 'widening participation opportunity' when the very profession that we thought would 'widen' was closing ranks, how were Band 4s referred to in the interview? 'Watered down Band 5s.' When I left the conference, I went for a long walk to try to make sense of it all. I've got to tell you all, I cried. I didn't want to, but as I walked through the park in the rain, hot tears mingled with the chilly drops of rain on my cheeks. Politics, economy and power. We are not engaged in politics so we are consistent footballs in the games of economy and power. I read some of Apple's (2013) work and I liked him, he was easy to read and said a lot of things that I could relate to. Though I'm not sure how some of his arguments sit with me, I count him credible because though he's a white professor, he's lived the struggle as a parent of a Black adopted son. Maybe it would be more accurate to say that he has insights into the struggle. There's no denying that he is white, privileged, male and a professor, therefore powerful right!

Through the work of Apple (2013) I came across the idea of 'affective equality'. Check this out:

> Affective equality is totally devoted to the affective system and to a thoughtful interrogation of the socio-political, ideological and personal relationships that do (or do not) provide and sustain, love and solidarity ... Affective equality, portrays and analyses the voices, the joy, the pain and dense realities of women and men engaged in activities associated with their labour of love, care and solidarity in richly detailed and insightful ways. (p. 16)

I, for one was hoping I would have experienced some 'affective equality' at university and from work-based learning in a health context. Now I'm wondering if because widening participation provisions fail to reorganise around the norms of 'affective equality, how dare it assert that it is 'widening PARTICIPATION'? My experience of this space has made me view education differently. I know it could be argued that I should have considered education before. But at this point, my Dad's voice echoes in my head, he would say, Nsoromma, nothing is done before the time!

I want to include two more quotes before I share my lived experience. Apple (2013) again:

> Education is not a neutral activity. It is ultimately connected to multiple relations of exploitation, domination and subordination and very importantly to struggles to deconstruct and reconstruct those relations. (p. 23)

For me, it is only now that we are deconstructing our educational experience that I'm even thinking like this. Apple also says, 'negative educational experiences have a damaging effect on both the sense of self and the understanding of what one can truly become' (p. 21). Well, after I read that quote, I dropped the book and couldn't pick it up again for a couple of days. In those days however, I thought a lot about my schooling and recalled the times teachers would tell me that I could never be the nurse I wanted to be. My Dad encouraged education at home, but at school I was usually bored. Teachers never listened when I said the work was too easy for me ... I better leave those thoughts there! Though I acknowledge I'll need to revisit them as I journey towards self-liberation. Anyway, regarding getting through, I'm no longer sure, I want to say I got through ... got through what?

Any rode, here it goes: for the first couple of months just getting used to HE, you know it was exciting because I thought to myself it's a new thing. I'll get a bigger qualification out of this, meet new people and then it was just like the work load hit. It's so much assignments, everything was getting done but I thought it was just like one assignment after another and just before the end of the year ... the first year, it was like I had problems with a parent being ill and I couldn't concentrate. It was like uni's focus has gone out the window 'cause I needed to concentrate on my parent but I still got the work in. What knocked me, was exams. I'm not good at exams but I tried. I think they gave me three goes, I thought I had completed two goes and I had another go. However, I think with having all this pressure with my parent, I lost track ... they told me that I had 'failed' three attempts and I couldn't carry on with the course. I did explain to them the situation of my parent being ill and passing away and blah, blah but to me it was like ... 'oh well, you "failed" the course now, bye – see you later'. I didn't feel I was getting any support or anything.

When I 'failed' the first time, I don't think I really got much support. Just more like 'oh you've 'failed' the first exam, so ... well I had a few of my friends on the course so we tried to get in little groups and help each other out and stuff which sometimes worked. Practical's I'm fine but it's written exams. We had degree students that came on placement, they even said 'why is your course so hard, we've never had anything like this?' Their booklets were easier than ours and I thought, my gosh! So ... that kind of put me off a bit but I carried on, it's just that I felt like I did not get support.

I think when it got to the case of 'oh well, you've "failed" the course' and then I'm asking well how can I appeal and stuff? They said, 'well you've got to fill out this form and that form.' I thought I've never done this before, this is a new thing to me. They don't guide you ... to me, and I'm not being funny, but to me it felt like looking at my colour and saying 'naah, sod ya' because I am not the first person. There's a few ... there's a couple of Afro-Caribbean girls that have been on the course before and on my course that have really felt like that too.

If Dad were here now, I imagine he would be listening to my retelling with that quizzical look on his face and ask, Nsoromma, think ... who failed here? He would probe me about how I came to accept and repeat the institution's label of myself as a 'failure'. It was Dubois (1973) who said,

> educational establishments too often take on as teachers those of books and brains with no contact or firsthand knowledge of real everyday life and ordinary human beings ... those types of teachers generally fail. (p. 109)

In the crease of the page, I responded with a question, fail who though sir? Do they fail themselves, their students or both and how comes I've never heard in my lived experience of a lecturer/teacher failing their students? Anyway ... when I spoke to Sankofa, she challenged me to read up on the education of our generation, so I guess I'll find some examples.

I was told I'd been withdrawn and stuff like that. I appealed, it's just like a waiting game and then they reject you. They said I lost the appeal, so I thought fine, I've lost the appeal, get my head together. I did my assignments, yes, but that's what's really frustrating as well ... I passed the assignments but when it got to the exam, because I 'failed' the exam they did not want to carry me on. But I thought you could have at least said 'oh well, carry on the next year and we'll do the exam at the end or something, but no'. I'm not convinced my personal experience was taken into consideration, the process seemed to be nothing more than a formality. I exited university wondering why I wasn't exposed to the educational experience that DuBois (1973) had envisioned when he wrote:

> an educator should be far more than a master of a branch of human knowledge. They have got to be able to impart their knowledge to human beings whose place in the world is today precarious and critical; and possibilities and advancement of

that human being in the world where he is to live and earn a living is of just as much importance in the teaching process as the content of the knowledge taught. (p. 105)

How could either the university or NHS Trust argue that what I was exposed to was even an 'opportunity'? It could be argued that they considered what should be taught, but failed to consider the whom and the how. Sorry, guys, I can feel myself getting annoyed again so I'm going to sign off here. In conclusion, my partner and kids were great, they understood that I had this 'opportunity' and the work had to be done. They were really supportive. Ladies, looking forward to next time.'"

Sankofa: (Reflective – walks back to her chair and sits.)

GyeNyame: 'Time for a comfort break and a brew? Don't know about anyone else, but I'm ... I don't know what I am ... how could something appearing to be right, you know the offer of a free foundation degree, go so wrong? Universities need more of their staff to engage in critical pedagogies. Anyway ... time for some music I think. SunSum, can you be the selector?'

(SunSum walks over to the iPad and picks Jimmy Cliff's many rivers to cross ... the lyrics commence: 'Many rivers to cross, but I can't seem to find my way over, wondering I am lost, as I travel along ...')

The women sit and chatter as GyeNyame and Nsaa serve hot milky drinks and nibbles. The atmosphere is energised with outbursts of laughter.

Mama B: (Shouts above the chatter.) 'Just giving you a heads-up, ladies, we will start again in five minutes.'

SunSum: (Swaying to the music, rises, reaches over to the iPad and switches off the music.)

Mama B: 'Okay, ladies, we've heard the voices of two of our absent friends and we can see that their reading is contributing to sense making. How shall we proceed?'

(Nsaa jumps to her feet, with book and notepad in hand.)

Nsaa: 'My experience was somewhat positive so maybe I should go next and offer another perspective. Well, let me start by saying, I consider what we are doing here to be REAL education. I'm really enjoying our engaging with concepts and ideas, loving it! I get the feeling that we are all enjoying Freire, so I'll start with one of his quotes:

> an education that was not connected to the struggles for emancipation and against exploitation was not worthy of the label education. (Freire 1987: p. 24)

I think our absent friends have demonstrated the absence of "affective equality" in their accounts. In addition, I question whether what our sisters experienced was education at all. I think they made some powerful points exposing the deficits in universities and the NHS, structures. These institutions often boldly declare the rhetoric of equality, inclusion and social justice but the reality is rarely experienced by the minority groups they claim they want to reach.

The question is ... will they ever get there? Sankofa encourages us to go back, learn from the past, then move on. Here's my tentative attempt!

Many years ago, I went and done a course which really inspired me ... it was sort of, the first time I think I identified myself as a Black woman. I think, what it was, the people that were there were sharing the same kind of stories. And it was targeted at Black women, some of dual heritage as well but all identifying as Black women. The course was taught by Black women, but with one white tutor. But, erm, she was aware or understanding, I don't know if it was aware or understanding or a bit of both. I don't know if they discussed this but certain things she just wouldn't come in to. Yeah, certain discussions she just wouldn't come in to. That's because she knew that her presence would restrict us expressing ourselves, so that was good.

It was a Black project and that actual building was, erm, Marcus Garvey. So, we observed certain things that Marcus Garvey stood for, they would keep that tradition so ... so, I worked ... Yeah, erm, so I was there for a while and again it was a very Black environment and that place was set up to get young women, Black women back into employment and education. The organiser was a very militant, red skin woman, you will still see her around now, if you go to any kind of cultural venues or cultural events. She will be there pumping the Black power, and then there was J ... she was a Black woman again ... Now that education was about collectively and individually drawing out our strengths, I'm telling you, as bell hooks (1981) advocates: "both the teachers and us students recognised that we were all responsible for creating the learning environment together." As a result, our sessions were incredibly powerful and useful. Through bell hooks' work I can now describe what I experienced there as "engaged pedagogy". bell hooks (1981) suggests that engaged pedagogy occurs when:

> there is a mutual relationship between teacher and students that nurtures the growth of both parties, creating an atmosphere of trust and commitment ... she asserts that engaged pedagogy makes better learners because it asks us to embrace and explore the practice of knowing together, to see intelligence as a resource that can strengthen common good. (p. 22)

So, I feel well and truly blessed to be experiencing "engaged pedagogy" again here too.

So, ladies ... what got me through the fd ... was me ... my determination ... I had a positive academic Black woman in my department who was willing to guide me. I hadn't been in education for years ... and you know, you tend to gravitate don't you ... to your own?

But I walked into the room at university, had a quick scan around the room and I thought ... where's the black people? I did ... so anyway ... there were several things I didn't realise when we first started ... I just use to go to the sessions and I was waiting to be directed ... 'cause that's what I was used to ... being directed. I thought I've made my first step now ... I'm at university ... anyway, I'm going through and after about a month or so ... the other students were asking ... oh, have you started your workbooks? I thought ... workbooks ... which workbooks? So, I said to my colleague have you started your workbooks? ... She said no ... so obviously ... that's when I learned it was self-directed ... you must direct yourself! I've got to say, I had to shift gears quickly. I went out, got diaries and highlighters and planned and planned. I also realised that I had to get the family on board very early on. We had to get better at communicating and planning. Keeping it real, my children helped me a lot through university.'

Akoben: 'Hang on a minute, Nsaa, so what effect did the self-directed learning have on you getting to grips with uni and how did you manage the self-directed aspect?'

Nsaa: 'As I've said I'd been exposed to some teachers whose approach to teaching had been quite radical and transformative. I think that is probably why the idea of going to uni didn't faze me really. But I must say, widening participation offered me the hope of something new, something ideal for the mature, working student. I think it was

Giroux (1987) who said that even those with ideological conventions ignore the complexity and foundational relation between student culture and learning. He went on to say that, "some teachers' best intentions are subverted by employing a pedagogy that is part of the very dominant logic they seek to dismantle" (p. 19). So, to answer your question Akoben, I was floored by the whole idea of self-directed learning at first. I was a non-participant because I didn't understand the concept and I felt totally disempowered and marginalised because it seemed that I was the only one who didn't get it. I must quickly add that I wasn't and after getting over the shock that I was behind some of my peers, I soon educated myself and caught up.

My support, guidance and inspiration was me wanting to complete and my kids ... I think my biggest inspiration after getting in and seeing what it required of me was to self-motivate to complete. I talked to myself, Nsaa ... if you just push yourself a little bit more ... you could get top marks in everything ... because I wasn't pushing myself ladies ... I'll be honest. My self-determination got me through ... more than anything. I've got this book ... *Waris Dirie* [*Desert Flower*] ... and I bought it to show you today ... I think before I started that course or roundabout ... I was reading this book and it was probably one of the first books I completed cover to cover. She inspired me, 'cause she went through so much and still achieved. I thought ... I'm just gonna go for it ... but as I said ladies ... once I get onto something ... I ain't gonna stop it ... and I know even if I am under immense pressure ... I will still carry on ...

Having listened to my sisters I am now asking myself if my previous "custom-made" education had enabled me to "survive" the structures we work and access for vocational education. If I return to Freire (1978) he wrote about educators using descriptions such as "traditional" and "liberating" and he said that neither had "the right to deny the students' goals for technical training or job credentials" (p. 68). What I'm learning here is that the traditionalist is concerned with preserving the "establishment" and their approach means that the dominant group is always in power. I think it was also Giroux's (1987) idea that "to be educated is not to be free, it is to be present and active in the struggle for reclaiming one's voice, history and future" (p. 11). Listening to Nsoromma's piece, I was reminded that liberating approaches to education, "avoids blaming the students." She was taught using conventional styles, she didn't grasp the subject well enough to get the grades to pass, then she had no support, yet she's the one who "failed!" Enough said!'

SCENE 6

                    (She collects her notes which are scattered on the floor and returns to her chair.)

Sankofa: 'Thanks, Nsaa, I'm heartened by some of the points coming out of these conversations. I'm encouraged that you have really engaged with the wide range of authors. Now, Mama B and I had a conversation at the start of our meeting.

       The thing about being in the comfort of a home means we can lose all sense of time ...'

GyeNyame: (Interrupts, stands to her feet and declares:) 'I hope you are not going to suggest that we close here Sankofa. We were also talking over coffee, and we can't believe how cathartic this is, thanks for the word, Nsaa. So if you and Mama B are okay for time we need to have a form of semi-closure on this tonight. I mean we would like to at least air the thoughts we've had pent up since the conference.'

Sankofa: 'Does GyeNyame speak for everyone?'

Akoben: 'Yes, she does, and I would like to suggest that we put some low music on in the background this will help to lift us a little, we want to continue but sometimes it's a little heavy.'

Mama B: 'I'll be honest ladies, though I'm enjoying what is happening here. I need to go ... When a home was suggested, I thought, uh oh, the setting tends to impact discipline. I've had a long day and would really appreciate it if you could call me a cab please, GyeNyame. It is nine thirty. It's a shame because I know I'm going to miss out ... goodnight, ladies.'

(The room is quiet. No one responds. Mama B rises and walks to the door. She locates her coat and starts to put it on.)

(GyeNyame rises and follows behind Mama B. GyeNyame is visibly disappointed by Mama B's desire to leave.)

GyeNyame: (Whispers.) 'It's okay, Mama B, we wondered whether you would be in this for the long haul like us. Sometimes things don't go to plan but we must keep going ... that's our lived experience. We are silenced in uni, silenced at work, we rarely come together to share. In fact, I must admit even we are surprised at our commitment to this, especially with all the reading we have had to be doing ... I guess not all of us need to fully commit though, eh?'

(Sankofa walks into the hallway and interrupts GyeNyame, who is in full flow.)

If only we had known

Sankofa:	'Is everything ok?'
GyeNyame:	(Ignoring Sankofa's question, continues speaking to Mama B.) 'You said we were in this together, then on the first occasion that we are off script ... you're off. Are we not making quick enough progress for you? Are we not getting to grips with the academic stuff at a level that stimulates you? I'm sorry, but I jolly well dared to believe that we could see this thing through together. It would be a first on so many levels. But hey, I'll get your cab. We always say that those who have arrived ... generally don't have patience with those on the journey. We kind of hoped you and Sankofa were different.'
Mama B:	(Addresses Sankofa.) 'Yes, everything's fine. My sister here is questioning my commitment. She's having her say ...'
Mama B:	(Addresses GyeNyame.) 'I know how my leaving may look to you GyeNyame. But I need to let you know that your accusations are quite unfair. Our commitment to do something different in this space, to address a seat of injustice is just one of the many "battles" I am COMMITTED TO. I'm fully aware of what our people say about people who they perceive have "arrived". I want to remind you that from the start of the journey, I made it clear that I was in the struggle. I haven't arrived anywhere and I am disappointed and somewhat annoyed by your tone. However, I'm glad you had the courage to voice how you perceive things as this enables dialogue which hopefully leads to a better understanding. It was Lorde (2007) who said, "what is most important to me must be spoken, made verbal and shared, even at the risk of having it bruised or misunderstood" (p. 40). I guess that's where WE are! So, forget the cab GyeNyame, yo' made yo' point, I don't agree with a lot of what you said, but our tensions, suspicions, and past assumptions will all need to be part of navigating this space. I'll make a call home and I'll return to the group.'

(GyeNyame visibly shaken returns to the room where Darius Rucker's song 'This' (2011) oozes softly from the iPad.)

> For every stoplight, I didn't make
> Every chance I did or I didn't take
> All the doors that I had to close
> All the things I knew but I didn't know
> Thank God for all I missed
> Cause it led me here to
> This ...

(The aroma of Jamaican Blue Mountain coffee permeates the air. The women are deep in hushed conversations, then suddenly, the door opens. The talking stops and all eyes shoot towards the door. With beaming smiles, they welcome Mama B back into the room.)

Mama B: (Jovially.) 'An' you lot can shut down those Cheshire cat grins ... now if I'm staying I need to have a go at giving you an insight into my world.'

(There's cheering, clapping and a light laughter that's contagious. Try as she might not to laugh, Mama B is also infected and she finds herself laughing alongside the others.)

(GyeNyame pours Mama B a mug of coffee, winks and mouths, 'thank you'.)

(Mama B stands behind her seat, clears her throat and recites a prose.)

Mama B: '"When you see me, you think, you see arrived and free, but I know different, I've lived this whole trajectory

You see me all dolled up and looking good, but,

you have not seen the multiple, oppressive wounds I've withstood,

you hear of the triumphs, but I've lived through each scar,

you think that I've accomplished, but I know, I've only come so far,

I can't carry the world, though so often I feel I do.

The problem with carrying the world is, who the hell then carries you?

I feel the weights of race and gender sitting heavily on my shoulders,

I despair because there's so few of us that navigate the institutional boulders.

Sometimes I just want to have space to be me and grow,

But I know I must be here for others, who have no one else but us few, to turn to, or to go!" Thank you!'

Nsaa: 'Wow ... Off the cuff? Love it! I think that deserves a round of applause, ladies.'

(The women rise to their feet and applaud.)

If only we had known 65

GyeNyame: 'You're spot on, Mama B.'
Mama B: (Looks directly at GyeNyame and winks.) 'A few minutes ago, GyeNyame, when she was sharing her mind, mentioned being silenced. I heard her voice break as she choked back the pain. I want to speak into that pain for a few moments. When Black feminist activist Audre Lorde reflected on her life following a cancer diagnosis she wrote that amongst the things she most regretted was her silence. Now, I wouldn't say she was silent at all, she had a lot to say and indeed she said a lot of profound things leaving a legacy of "knowing" for generations to come. However, she knew the fear associated with speaking out. In her reflection of engaging in civil rights Lorde (2007) identified herself "not only as a casualty" but also as a "warrior". She said that: "learning to put fear into perspective gave her great strength". Lorde was a believer that her silences hadn't protected her and neither would ours. Lorde told a story about a conversation she had with her daughter on the topic of silence and her daughter's response impacted me personally. Listen to what her daughter said: "there's a little piece of you that wants to be spoken out, and if you keep ignoring it, it gets madder and madder and hotter and hotter and if you don't speak it out, one day it will just up and punch you in the mouth from the inside" (Lorde 2007: 42).'

(There's an eruption of laughter, slapping of thighs, heads nodding and on each face, there's that look of knowing.)

Mama B: (Continues.) 'Finally, Lorde said: "For we have been socialised to respect fear more than our needs for language and definition, and while we wait in silence for that final luxury of fearlessness, the weight of silence will choke us" (Lorde 2007:44). So, GyeNyame, maybe our little tay ta tay in the hallway was part of your initial steps to using your voice … to breaking silence. I'm sure this is a subject we will come back to. Because of time I'll park that thought. Akoma, are you ready?'
Akoma: 'Wow, Mama B. How in the world do I follow that? So, glad you decided to stay. I would have hated to have lost out on that poem and thought. We got that powerful contribution, all because, GyeNyame spoke out.'
GyeNyame: (Reflective.) 'All because the words punched me in the mouth from the inside.'

As the words leave GyeNyame's mouth, the room is once again lightened by laughter.

Akoma: 'It was interesting listening to Nsoromma's account, 'cause we were told we had four attempts at the exam, so the message on exams was not consistent. I failed twice. I went and spoke to the tutor and asked her what areas I should revise, she was little help as she just told me to revise everything we covered. And, why do they make the language so highbrow anyway? I got through because one of my colleagues on the course said, "ok Akoma, I'll meet up with you and we'll cover such and such a' area". So, she met with me twice. I got the diagrams, I was struggling with an' then stuck them on the wall, so that as soon as I came in, I saw it and made the link, oh yes, that's what that means. I began to tape myself and I had the tapes so that I could listen to them as I went along ...

I'm telling you, everyone on the course had sleepless nights because we didn't know what hit us! You know, because with everything we were just thrown in at the deep end. We were told, "oh, it's a foundation degree" and that's it. We never really got the support. I mean, at the hospital we had a little crash course errm ... but you know, we needed a better level of support than we had. We all were amateurs; we'd never been to university before so we never understood the university language or culture. So, we could have done with more of a ... what did Nsoramma call it ... affective equality from those at the university. Whereas you know, we were never really given that. You know, we didn't get as much help as we should at work either. It's like you're off the ward a little time and the nursing team expect you to know everything. They are wanting to delegate asking "Oh can you do this?" When I said, I can't, they'll, then say, "Oh you've been to the course, what have you been doing?" I readily reminded them that within nursing you cannot go and complete a procedure that you haven't been trained to do. They didn't make the link that if they didn't train me, I can't do the task.

Well, it would have been nice if I had completed the course. But, errm, you know, with the support ... I didn't have that. Because even if you're doing something and you're stuck on it. You don't always get the help either to complete it. I've always asked, because as I say, the worse one can say is no. So, it's not like I didn't ask but when you work on a busy ward and nurses are busy it's very, very hard to get the practical training. I was constantly reminded that I was not an equal to student nurses, you know, you must be hanging around and you don't get the help.

I ... to be honest, I don't think I've failed. If I had gone into the second year and hadn't passed anything at all then I would have considered that a failure. Whereas as I say, it was because of circumstances why I didn't end up completing it. But I wouldn't really class it as a failure, would be lovely to say that I received the degree but it's just one of those things. So, I'll try to tell you how my reading links into my experience. I had a book by Dewey, I enjoyed it so much. I tell you ladies, I marked up that book, at times it felt like fire in my hands. There were times when he wrote of my experience so clearly, I literally just froze. I'm being serious. This kind of reading and engaging with text is new to me and so empowering. Yes, Nsaa, it's transformative!

The university, knew we were not what they refer to as "traditional" students. We had come the vocational route, yet they never varied their assessments for our programme of study. They "transmitted", but we couldn't work out the body of information. We needed support in further developing our skills to confidently work at the HE level. The uni and work maintained what Dewey described as the "pattern of organisation", in other words, the way they use lecture theatres, classrooms, time schedules, schemes of examinations and promotion of rules, like if you "fail" your exam so many times you're off the course and so on. But "pattern of organisation" disadvantages and silences "non-traditional" students. We don't know, because we were not taught the rules. Yet for those who make and are gatekeepers of the rules it's business as usual. It sometimes felt like the university's structures were saying. We took you in, didn't we? What more do you want? You're here now ... fit in with our way or take the highway. We've done our bit. Many us just couldn't fit into a way that was never originated with us in mind and refused to adapt to accommodate us!

I mean Nsoromma's experience was "pattern of organisation" those inflexible patterns led to her being ejected from the course! Dewey (1997), in his criticism of "traditional education", states: "The traditional scheme is, in essence, one of imposition from above and from outside" (p. 18). So, although they labelled us "non-traditional" students, we were treated no differently to the so-called "traditional students".

Now, if the truth be known, there is a gulf between the academic experience and abilities of "traditional" and "nontraditional" mature students and the university and NHS Trust knew that. Why were we governed by the same standards? I have said that I don't think I failed and that's because I think that both institutions prohibited my active participation because of their business as usual approach to providing me with a so-called opportunity. I'm not stupid and I'm disciplined so I could have completed if the institutions had enabled me to. Prior to entry they offered me support, which didn't manifest.

In conclusion, if we are to believe what Mmara said in her interview, neither the university or the workplace had a "well thought-out philosophy of social factors that operate in the constitution of individual experience" (Dewey, 1997: 20). If I speak for the absent sisters as well as myself, we didn't engage in transformative education designed to meet our needs. We were violated by historical systems and structures which wanted us to fit our size seven abilities, knowledge and exposure into their size three institutional provisions. It couldn't work for many of us and we should not have had to live it, to prove it. The university is filled with academics who allegedly know about how education works. But do they know? The NHS is filled with nurses who are qualified assessors and mentors but do they care? I'll be re-reading Dewey and maybe returning to his works in future meetings. Sorry, but this level of reflection is very new to me though it's tough to look injustice in the face and name it, I'm moving from the stage of merely being peed off by it, I'm building the resilience to question it in a different way. Guys, I really do love this space! Wanna take over, SunSum?'

SunSum: 'Would you all mind if I just put a song on? This is for all of us in this room and all the mature students who will come behind us, whatever their colour or background can we just let it play out ...'

(She walks around the plates on the floor to the sideboard and selects the Hollies song, 'He ain't heavy, he's my brother'.)

> The road is long
> With many a winding turn
> That leads us to who knows where
> Who knows where
> But I'm strong
> Strong enough to carry him

If only we had known 69

> He ain't heavy, he's my brother
> So, on we go
> His welfare is of my concern
> No burden is he to bear
> We'll get there
> For I know
> He would not encumber me
> He ain't heavy, he's my brother ...

(After a complete round, only the odd sniffle intermittently interrupts the silence.)

(GyeNyame hands around the box of tissues and tears are slowly wiped away. Everything seems to be happening in slow motion.)

(Tears and tensions are released as the words of the song wash over those in the room like a balm.)

> If I'm laden, at all
> I'm laden, with sadness
> That everyone's heart
> Isn't filled with the gladness
> Of love for one another ...

(SunSum walks over and stops the song in mid flow ... the room is silent again.)

GyeNyame: (Breaking the silence.) 'Ladies, would you mind if I prayed? I'm going to read a variation of a short prayer by Nordette N. Adams (2013). Heavenly father, "open our hearts to accept the one called 'other' who seems so unlike those we prefer to call sister or brother. Open our eyes to see the illusions of social hierarchy. Help us overcome the smaller mind that divides and conquers humankind. Amen."

Thank you, ladies, prayer is one of my tried and tested de-stressors. Though that was a little heavy, it was good, I feel like we're getting somewhere. What do I mean? Well, Akoma is right, the university and the NHS Trust should have known that this seemingly unthought-through provision would provide a bitter sweet experience. But I know from all my conversations with Sankofa that we need to take some responsibility. Now don't get me wrong this is not about blame. This is about us, educating ourselves on our histories that though the institutions suffer from amnesia, we really can't afford to!

If we had done our research, had knowledge of our parents' histories, then I wonder how different our experience would have been. Wouldn't it have been something if collectively, armed with the insights we have now, we had gone to the institutions with questions about how they were going to ensure we had a positive educational experience? If we had asked our employers to enter into a contract with us to pay us for the skills we were developing, to provide us with assurance that we would be treated as students. In this space, we are arming ourselves for the next, so-called, new initiative and hopefully we will be ready to be less "grateful recipients" and more "critical negotiators". SunSum it's over to you.'

SunSum: (Facing Sankofa.) 'I hope I'm not out of line here, but Sankofa, we haven't heard much from you. I'm prepared to go next, but I wondered if you could share some of what's on your mind. You were either part of our preparation for the fd or our support whilst we were on the fd. I don't know if you know this but women of all backgrounds talk about you a lot in our snatched moments in clinical settings. People you teach, enjoyed learning with you and we wondered if our experiences and outcomes would have been different if the lecturers were more like you in style. I, for one, remember that it was in your classes that I and others like me first read Black authors in an educational setting. I never even read the works of Black people at school. Can you remember how emotional I got when you first introduced us to Mary Seacole in Literacy Level 2? I'm not ashamed to say this, though maybe I should be, I cried in the class and I asked Sankofa why had I never heard of this woman and I even did an access to nursing course? Those sessions produced lively discussions. They were fab. I also learned that important lesson on the difference between criticising and critical analysis. See if you agree with me ladies, as Black kids, to criticise was forbidden, our parents would give us a good telling off for criticising. True?'

(The women respond agreeing with SunSum.)

'That critical analysing malarkey, took some getting my head round. You got us telling our stories and you shared them in journals and at conferences. I know you have spoken to each one of us on the journey, but this space was your idea. How are you feeling now and could you share some of your thoughts with us?'

Sankofa: 'If the truth be known, SunSum, I'm tired and as emotional as everyone else right now. Or perhaps, even more so. Firstly, you are not out of line, okay! As the prayer GyeNyame read stated, any perceived hierarchy here is merely an illusion. I'm in this, not as a lead but as one on her own journey. I've been busy trying to capture all the remarkable stuff that's being unveiled in these spaces. Well ... where do I start? I think I want to have a go at speaking into some of the things that have come out so far. As I'm not prepared it may be disjointed, but I'll try to link as much as I can.

First, let me just "out" a thought and leave it in the air. We say our parents told us not to criticise. I wonder where our parents, who were brought up under a colonial system, learnt not to criticise? Was there a colonised hierarchy of power attached to their understanding of criticism, and is that what resulted in the forbiddance? Now we don't have time to go there right now ... but it is a question worth considering. Now let me return to the space. We have started explorations into: breaking silence, power dynamics in educational settings, how economy and education are linked as well as using our knowledge to critically engage. We are also exploring a range of intentionally inclusive approaches to pedagogy.

The words transform and transformation have been recurrent in our space, so I'll pick up on that theme first ... bell hooks (1981) advocates that: "when she learns about her students, she knows how better to serve them in the role of an educator". That's my belief too. I assure you that me introducing Black authors into work-based literacy did not go unnoticed by my Caucasian colleagues. I got my share of criticism, but to be honest, I didn't have to argue hard to silence the critics. I merely exposed the fact that I was addressing the lack of diversity in our resources. I hope that through your encounter with me as an educator you observed me proactively dismantling the hierarchical structure. I acknowledge that I may have had some "power" as the tutor in the classroom but in my eyes, we are all on a similar journey towards social justice through a critiquing of the dominant culture. But let me not hide my own shortcomings. The very concept that precipitated this journey we are on was how I interpreted "failure". I started this study because ... some of you were "failures" and I was questioning whether I had, in part, contributed to you being "failures" ... I know ... can you believe I thought like that? How naive!

I had subconsciously accepted the institutions' labelling of some of you as failures. I too, was a victim of "colonised thinking". Woodson (1933) contends that: "only by careful study of the 'negro' himself and the life which he is forced to lead can we arrive at the proper procedure of education" (p. xiv). He further argues that: "the mere imparting of knowledge is not education." I think Akoma pointed that out when she referred to Dewey's work too. Woodson was radical in his approach to education and through his work, and the work of many others, I was supported in my long-winded journey to a different epistemology.'

(She writes on the whiteboard on her lap then holds it up so others can read the words.)

The road is long with many a winding turn, that leads us to who knows where, who knows where.

Sankofa: (Continues.) 'My programme of study is a six-year programme if you're lucky. I'm just over half way in and yes, the road has been winding. Most of the time, I ask myself ... what possessed you to take this on? You see, I am the first of my siblings to go to university too. I'm driven by three things predominantly: passion, purpose and principle. Once I got on the course and realised that not completing was not an option for me. I then had the challenge of trying to find out how to engage on this academic course in a manner that wasn't going to leave me feeling like I had used you to get to an academic height and leave you in your uncontested places. So, this is a risk ... I have lost count of the number of people who have advised me against taking a non-traditional approach. But I spoke to my supervisors as well as my very wise father. He reminded me that every choice or decision ever worth taking is a risk and social justice issues are certainly risks worth taking.'

(She writes on the whiteboard on her lap again then holds it up so others can read the words.)

But I'm strong, strong enough to carry ~~him~~, her. She ain't heavy, she's my ~~brother~~ sister. So, on we go ...

'For the record, I don't feel strong, well not often enough. I feel like a fraud, yep, I suffer from imposter syndrome, but I've spoken to students from all backgrounds and walks of life, even those who may be labelled "traditional" who say they feel the same. For the past three years, I have lived between laughter and breakthrough

If only we had known 73

and tears and despondency. I cry because I don't feel strong enough to carry this mantle of doing things differently. Who the hell am I?

I don't want the responsibility of your voices. I don't want to carry the weight of race and gender everywhere I go. I cry often because I don't know enough, of the how to ... I cry because nothing ever seems constant ... I think I get a handle on "it", then I lose "it". I feel confident one minute and scared stiff the next. I feel somewhat confused. I laugh because I understand my privilege. I think, God, you're having a laugh to have placed me here for such a time as this. Reluctantly, I accept that I have been exposed to too much, so as Lorde (2007) said, I "cannot sit in my safe corner as a mute bottle" (p. 42). I must face my fears. It's my purpose and passion that fuel me to try and keep trying. I laugh when I leave a supervision and my supervisors can see the points I'm trying to make, even if my attempt is somewhat clumsy at the first, second and third drafts. I laugh because on very few odd days ... I do feel strength rising and I seek out sources to keep it topped up.'

(She writes on the whiteboard on her lap again then holds it up so others can read the words.)

~~His~~ Her welfare is my concern, no burden is she to bear, we'll get there, for I know, she would not encumber me, she ain't heavy, she's my ~~brother~~ sister.

Sankofa: 'I want to do this for us, so it will take approximately five or so years of my life. It will cost me thousands of pounds. But what choice do I have? I could have closed my eyes and thanked God that I don't live with the day-to-day disparagements that you have inflicted on you. I could have aligned myself with the institutions and become "colour blind". I could have carried on blaming you for "failing". But way too many have done that! I didn't want to be part of that school. So, our welfare, and the educational welfare of generations to come is my concern. You know something, I don't go to classes and stuff now, I work a lot in isolation so it's tough and the dreams in my head are just dreams. Or so I thought ... what we are doing now, is living my dream. It is my hope and dream that what results from our space will influence, inspire and impact people of all backgrounds, but I want this work to be accessible to Black people. When I shared with my father what I wanted to do and how scared I was because I was swimming against the tide, he reminded me of these lines.

> Your playing small does not serve the world.
> There is nothing enlightened about shrinking so that other people won't feel insecure around you.
> We are all meant to shine, as children do.
> We were born to make manifest the glory of God that is within us.
> It's not just in some of us; it's in everyone.
> And as we let our own light shine, we unconsciously give other people permission to do the same.
> As we are liberated from our own fear, our presence automatically liberates others. (Marianne Williamson, 1992)

As I've listened to the recollections and reflections, so much of what you have experienced has been written about in a study I recently read by Miriam David. I heard Nsaa assert, we had no higher education role models. Hockings, Cooke and Bowl (2010) found that students who were first in their families to attend universities heavily relied on tutors or managers to guide them on the 'right' path. So, you had no expectation that others in your situation didn't have. You expected those leading to have your best interests at heart. I also heard Akoma agonising over the fact that though you were "non-traditional" students yet the only form of pedagogy you were exposed to were the traditional styles. Well, Hockings et al. (2010) found that to be true in a study they undertook. They stated:

> Research on the impact of widening participation found little evidence that teaching methods had been adapted to meet the changes in the composition of the student population. (p. 95)

End of quote. So, you see, it's not appropriate or fair to use the word "failure" to describe students until we start exploring what happens in the institutions.

In the study I just mentioned, they also explored how teachers academically engaged all students within a culturally, socially and educationally diverse classroom. Following their exploration, they found that:

> over three quarters of the teachers they studied admitted they knew very little about the lives, backgrounds and interests of their students.

Yet they all distanced themselves from the deficit view of "non-traditional" student. (p. 101)

How could I continue to uncritically label you as "failures" when you inform me that teachers seemed unwilling to rephrase the points they were trying to get across and would rather repeat even though you stated you did not understand the first time? David (2010) in her study of widening participation students found that:

> they found it hard to stay engaged during lectures. They wanted analogies, stories and illustrations. (p. 105)

Now it would be too easy to simply blame the teachers, we have come further than that, haven't we? We understand that institutional policies, targets and inspections are probably contributors to making 'transformative approaches' to learning too risky for teachers. Akoma, I loved the way you picked up Nsoromma's phrasing of her experience after she failed her exams. You both used the words "ejected". Vignoles and Powdtharee (2010) in their exploration of institutional policies used the term 'forced withdrawal' to describe the process for those who had to leave a course following an exam failure. I don't want to pre-empt what others may be saying after me yet, I recall some of you telling me, much to my frustration at the time, that lecturers had informed you that you could exit the course at year one as you would still get the cap and gown. I recall arguing with you saying, quite assertively, that you could get the cap and gown and a full qualification at the end of the second year too. In my quiet moments, I have wondered if lecturers were encouraging you to "voluntarily withdraw" because it was their perception that you were incapable of completing year two.

Finally, I am encouraged by your resilience. David et al. (2010) argue that:

> disadvantaged students demonstrated greater resilience and commitment to their studies, often in the face of adverse structural discrimination and oppression. (p. 153)

In this space, you are sharing your strategies for survival ... it's insightful and I'm sure the half has not been told. In closing, Woodson (1933) suggests that:

> real education means to inspire people to live more abundantly, to learn to begin with life as they find it and make it better. (p. 29)

	Well, I don't know about you but I get new hope bubbling up in me after each of these sessions as I think that is exactly what we are striving to do. To paraphrase Woodson, philosophers have long conceded that every wo/man has two educations, that which is given to him/her and the other that he/she gives her/himself. In this space, we are educating our self and from what I can see, we're doing a good job and as importantly, we're loving it! How's that, SunSum, can I stop there for now?'
SunSum:	'I'm glad I called on you now, you would have gone home with that … now I want to read Woodson. Thanks. Another quick comfort break before …'

(Mid-sentence, the women head towards the door and head in differing directions. Some to the kitchen, others to the upstairs and downstairs loos.)

GyeNyame:	(Heads back to the living room, tray in hand.) 'Tea's up …'

(The women make their way back to the living room and take their seats.)

| SunSum: | (Sits uprightly then commences.) 'I'll tell you the truth, I'm beginning to wonder, what I got myself into here? I thought what we call "the space" was just going to be conversations. Philosophising is psychological stuff and it's heavy. I can tell you this, I've learnt more in these sessions relevant to my life than I did in two years at university. I wish I could explain how I feel … Yes, Sankofa, I'm lovin' it! I share what we discuss here with my brother and he adds another perspective. He often reminds me that adult education should be enjoyed and should transform lives! My brother is quite political though; I don't often think of Black women as political, yet I wonder if what we are doing here is politics. I mean, even GyeNyame's, prayer was kinda political … anyway … my first year at university was hell. Erm, you were just thrown into things … not what I expected, erm … I go to the library and try to absorb everything and I'd leave giddy. I just couldn't absorb what they wanted or … did I even know what they wanted? It was really, really, tough. Felt like giving up loads of times … yeah, stopped an' cried and cried and cried … my husband … he'd say to me, yo' can do it. Yo' 'now, yo' clever … you can do it …

The compu … then because I wasn't good with the computer. I think that was my biggest problem. Yeah, we even had to use the |
|---|---|

computers to do forums ... I could do 'em ... 'cause I knew what I wanted to say ... but it was the IT bit. I'd never gone around a computer before doing that course, so everything was alien to me about computers and ... the kids were brilliant ... bared with me and showed me ... My husband was brilliant, he would say, don't give up. Erm, it was a lot ... it was a lot to take in with the assignments an' the workbooks, google. It was a lot an' ... if they had said, write a 3,000-word essay, I could do it with pen and paper no problem. Ah, research ... researching things, evidence-based, research, all that. It was just alien, it was just ... I was just thinking they should have introduced us to things a bit better, like, give us a month or two on how to be a mature student, because it was alien to me ... referencing, that was it, referencing and IT they were big issues for me.

One of the important lessons here for me, is to look at what is happening beyond us. I must say, I like Sankofa's honesty, but what stands out from what you said beyond your honesty Sankofa was that you were willing to delve further. We must, if we are to break the cycle of thinking that "it's us", that it's solely our fault, it's Black people and we can't get on in HE.

During the last break, Sankofa showed me two lines from the book she was quoting from and I thought. Oh, my word, so it wasn't us. Most of us were saying that student nurses were commenting that our course seemed intense with a lot more workbooks than even second year nurse students. Well please listen to this, Bathmaker (2010) found that fd programmes were not run any differently from Bachelor degree programmes. How can that be? It's shocking! I'm sure that there is more than one way of interpreting that sentence. But we have offered our perspective as well as some of our lived experiences ... then the institutions have the audacity to label us failures!

Bathmaker (2010) also found that some universities ran bridging programmes during the summer before the start of fd programmes. Those bridging programmes covered areas such as research skills, time management, taking notes, referencing and preparing presentations. So, what can we say, did the universities which failed to offer such support to their non-traditional students "fail" them? 'Course they did, at least they did in my humble opinion!

I got through because I met up with colleagues like Akoma and what she didn't know, I sort of helped her and she is good with the computer, so she helped me. It was just me and Akoma really ... you know, we helped each other. We got on the phone, we spoke an'

SCENE 6

... yeah, yeah ... if we didn't, we'd go potty. Yeah, you know what made you sort of down-hearted as well, the approach and attitude of the lecturers. One of the girls told me that she arrived early at the lecturer's office and heard the lecturer reading someone's work to another lecturer an' the two of them were laughing. Fancy lecturers jeering an' mecking fun of someone's efforts. Goes back to what Sankofa said, they didn't know us, our journey, neither did they seem interested in us. As students, we talk amongst ourselves an' everyone had the same sorta feelings. Err, what helped me through it as well, err, I've done physiology before so my way a coping wid dat, 'cause we had exams to teck.

I'd write stuff, stick it around on the walls ... get my brother to do big pictures, diagrams of the nervous system an' study it that way, an' I passed first time, an' I could not believe it. So, as you can see, my journey on the fd was a family affair and it is through the contributions and support of the family that I got through. That's all I wanted to add really.'

Akoben: 'Well, it's over to me, we've been going a while, so I'm gonna just say it as I saw it ... uni ... work-based learning, you know what ... it's just a big wide world and nobody gives a shit about ya. That's how I felt when I started ... I tell you the truth ... when I started uni ... everybody else seemed to know what they were doing. They were getting on with it ... I was like ... shit, so, what am I suppose' to do? You know ... all the talking ... I felt like it was doing this.

(With agitated facial expressions and one arm waving above her head.)

I remember talking to one of the tutors and she goes ... "Yea ... you're just feeling a bit bewildered ... it's new to you ... but it will come to you in time" ... which it did ... eventually, you know. This tutor goes ... there's a learning skills centre ... right ... there's people that would help you ... they won't write your assignment ... but they will help you with your assignment ... de referencing ... Lawd a gash ... Oh people, I'm telling ya ... the first year I found hard ... I had been so many years out of the education system ... having other commitments in life ... you know, my kids and what have you ... you know ... work as well and then taking this on ... it was really hard ... Determination got me through ... I knew I was gonna do it ... an' I heard my mum in my head ... yo' love start tings and no' finish dem ... I was finishing this ... I'm finishing this ... I'm finishing this ...

(Pauses to compose herself ... then recommences.)

When mi graduate an' when mi hab mi hat an' mi gown on ... you gonna see me crying ... you know ... cause I'm not doing it ... Yes ... I'm doing it for myself ...

(Loses her trail of thought, recomposes, then continues through her tears.)

I just wished she lived long enough to see me through and say Akoben ... An' yo' know what? I know my mum was proud of me ... I know she loves me ... but for this one time ... I could say, "see mum ... I started it ... and I finished it ..." You know what I mean ... so it doesn't matter how many hurdles ... I've got to jump ... I'm finishing this ... So if it takes me more than the two years ... then so be it ... I can still achieve and finish ... me a finish ... mi 'no' care.

You know ... I remember, I saw my manager in the corridor ...' cause she left us now ... she says ... "Oh Akoben, how's the course going?" an' I said ... it's going very well, thank you ... she says ... "Oh ... so what about everybody else?" I said ... oh, they all dropped out ... I'm the only one that's finishing ... an' mi smile and carried on walking ... and I thought ... yeah ... because you put everybody else ahead of me ... an' you know ... that's like another way ... of saying ... you weren't good enough ... to me ... I felt that ... you know what I mean ... I'm gonna put these people through ... because I think they are better than you ... Well, they weren't ... 'cause you know what ... dem nebba finish ... dem nebba finish ...

Going through the second year ... the workload was more ... the criteria to me was more stringent ... you know, it was like ... because when we first started for the first year ... the mistakes that you probably made ... they would overlook it ... and your referencing ... they didn't include it ... you had to do it ... but you weren't marked against it ... with the second year now ... everything was included ... so you had to do the referencing properly. Everything had to be right ... to get through the second year ... I mean the course itself was fine ... but we were meant to start the May ... clear inna July ... we still no start the course ... because the tutor was off sick ... So I'm saying to the course director ... so what ... only one tutor you have?

And then ... by the time ... they found somebody that could do that module ... they had left it so long ... our assignment hand in dates coincided ... So ... then you were trying to juggle everything ... I remember saying to the course director ... "This is too much ... This is too much because ... you know ... you're supposed to have time to just focus on one thing ... Yes ... you know ... you might end up juggling something at the end ... but three things ... she goes ...

well, you know, Akoben". I said, no, well, you know, Akoben, nuttun ... I says ... this is because the start date on this module was so late ... You know ... you have a deadline for your assignment ... right ... you hand it in ... then they give you a deadline to say ... well, you should get back your work at this time ... then they email you to say, "Oh, I wasn't able to look at your work, but you'll get it for this date". I remember the one module ... they delayed it and delayed it and by the time some of us got our assignment back ... the deadline for the resubmission was the following week ... assignments wha' yo' haffi write ... me sey ... lawd have mercy ... that was my challenge.

I remember asking before I started the course ... are there any exams? The response was NO ... I tell you ... if they had said to me ... you're gonna have to do an exam ... I would've said ... I don't want to do the course. I'm more of a hands-on person ... the pressure of revising and remembering ... doesn't work for me ... You know ... we're all different ... and no matter how ... I could read for the whole year ... you se' once mi si dun and de paapa look pon me ... blank! I doan se' a ting ... I had to go an' see Sully and let him give me some extra tuition for the exam because I just couldn't get my head around and the way they worded it you know ... You have to know what they're talking about to give the right answer ... well ... thank God ... I pass' the practical ... that was no problem ... but the written one ... I had to do it again ... But I pass' the next time ... my study partner was struggling and I just tell her ... me one naah go upon that stage ... me naah leave you ... you going up there with me ... I said, me and you have been here from start ... and we have ... my study partner and I met at work, in the library at the hospital ... in the library at the university ... she come a mi house ... mi go a fi har ... we've worked together.

Disciplining myself was my biggest challenge ... Not even ... I had a few run-ins with the course director and other tutors ... but that wasn't ... because you know what ... at the end of the day ... you don't have to like me ... you just need to teach me what I need to know ... but it was disciplining myself ... you know ... going to work ... coming home ... I'm tired ... all I want to do is go to my bed ... do you know how many all-nighters I've put in? I had to structure myself. I'm gonna be so honest with you ... life had to go on and work wasn't supportive either, I had to plead, don't put my nights so near to my uni days ... because if I have an assignment to do ... you know ... I've been up from day ... go right through to the night ... go right through to de next morning ... and just manage to hand in the assignment before 3 p.m.

If only we had known

I went to, what do they call it? PD something ... and there is a guy there and you would book in with him and he would ... I'm sure I saw it here somewhere (rummages around her reams of paper) because this critical analysing thing ... he was ever so good ... see it here ... this is all the writing ... he wrote down ... and I held onto that ... you know ... you think to yourself ... because it's all new to you ... everything just sounds difficult ...

But he just made it so clear ... I always hold on to this ... he did this over a year ago for me ... and I always hold on to it ... I just could not get it . ... What do you mean? Critically analyse what? And what are you talking about? But Ethan ... he was magic man ... I rate him ... I would go to him and he would say ... back again? ... and I would say ... yeah back again ... Yeah, he is good ... It's not been easy ... no, it's not been easy ... as mummy sey ... if yo' waan gud ... yo' nose haffi run ... there is good and bad in going to uni ... It is not just all bad ... I would not say it was all bad ... it is an uphill struggle ... I do not think that going to uni will ever be easy for us ... if it was easy, we would all do it. You know what I mean ... if it was easy ... everyone would do it ... and everyone would have their degree ... still no have no Band 4 job ... but you know ... that's my reflection. And yes, Mama B, I am going to get a mentor so I avoid slipping into stereotypical behaviours ... I think that I need to work on this going forward.'

Mama B: 'Thank you, Akoben. It would be great to pick up on some of these points. Akoben had a few things in common with other accounts, if I were to quickly summarise, disciplining herself was a challenge. Using her voice, she mentioned having run-ins with lecturers but importantly wanting to re-think how those run-ins happen. Finding it challenging to grasp what was taught, but then using support to gain enlightenment. There was a lot of good stuff there for exploration. Ladies, feel free to explore any one of those themes and share whether by email or telephone as you have been doing before or during our next session. Speaking of next session. Have we all got the next date in the diary? I will be hosting it at the university and I think you have requested that I invite a speaker. More information will follow. As usual, speak to Sankofa if you have any further points to raise or discuss. Now can we go home please? Mi tyard.'

(This time, there's no objection to closing the session. The women quickly assign themselves roles to wash up, fluff up cushions and tidy up the space they have just inhabited. Sankofa checks that the women have reading material before everyone heads out the doors.)

SCENE 7

Bittersweet realisation – hope we are the last

Final meet-up in the Frantz Fanon Lecture Theatre, 2nd floor in the University of Westmoreland

The first arrivals wait for the others in the staff car park where Mama B reserved parking spaces. For many, this campus setting makes them uncomfortable. As the group walk up the corridor they discuss some of the emotions racing around their minds and bodies: doubt, anxiety and fear. These emotions were both uninvited and unexpected so they choose instead to focus on aspects of resilience building, camaraderie and the fact that they now possess some insider knowledge.

They arrive at the lecture theatre which is spacious with large windows. Some head to the windows through which they see a range of sculptures, probably erected by students past and present. Akoben announces that the circle discussion, they had grown to love would never work in this space. On a large table at the front of the theatre was a finger buffet with an assortment of sandwiches, veg sticks, hot and cold drinks and fruit. The women looked at the display, totally unimpressed. They speak, but only hushed, undecipherable mutters can be heard. Sankofa appears distracted and disconnected from the group. She walks over to a large portrait of Franz Fanon hanging from the wall at the rear of the theatre, beneath the portrait is the following quote:

> The imaginary life cannot be isolated from real life, the concrete and the objective world constantly feed, permit, legitimate and found the imaginary. The imaginary consciousness is obviously unreal, but it feeds on the concrete world. The imaginary is possible only to the extent that the real world belongs to us. (Frantz Fanon, 1956 in Wildeman 2008: p. 1)

She reads the inscription to herself and then re-reads it aloud. Following the second reading, she reaches for her iPad, capturing the inscription in a photograph and mumbles to herself how incredible it is to find words spoken six decades ago which conceptualises her approach to academic writing in her time.

It is not long before chatter and laughter fills the room. This group of women have grown together, they weave in and out of each other's conversations. They are on epistemological and ontological journeys; they share their pride in what they are doing with heightened confidence that has grown out of their engagement. The initial emotions they experienced at entering the building seem to have abated.

Mama B appears, she looks flustered. She glances across at the food and mutters something about the absence of hot food. For a few minutes, she seems in a world of her own until Nsaa runs over to her and embraces her.

That embrace seems to free her from her deep thoughts and she emerges consciously into the space. She acknowledges the women, greeting each one by name with prolonged embraces.

> Sankofa: (Interjects.) 'Ladies, the session will commence in fifteen minutes.'

Some women head off in small groups to find the toilets, whilst others scrutinise the buffet removing the cling film. When the women return from the ladies, the whole group gathers unenthusiastically around the food, picking and complaining. After all, it is not what they are accustomed to.

> Akoben: 'Uno boycott de chicken, they still have the feathers on. Lawd, a bet dem no wash, nor season dem neither. Lawd, mi a go stick to de fruit an' de crisps.'
> GyeNyame: 'But a wha' Mama B do ya so. She 'no shudda know we betta dan dis? Bwoy, Mama B, you let we dung. An mi 'ungry yo' know. Wha' safe ya? The veg sticks and the crisps, maybe a couple a de sandwich.'
> Mate Masie: 'Uno bad sah ... bless an' eat, a so mi madda woulda sey.'

(The women pick around the food disdainfully, moving on to their seats with meagre helpings on plates.)

Mama B informs Sankofa that the speaker has not yet arrived.

Sankofa:	(Frustrated by lateness, selects the instrumental version of redemption songs by Bob Marley on the iPad, checks the speakers work, then joins the women.)
Mama B:	(Stands at the podium. The hubbub ceases.) 'Ladies, today we will commence with a song, please reach under your seats for the words. Whether you sing like angels or with no melody at all, it would be great if you would sing like no one was listening. Is that ok?'

The women down plates and search for the papers. At first glance, some immediately discard the paper as this is a song some know well.

Sankofa walks over to the iPad and turns it on. After the first few bars, the women start singing, and they sing with gusto from their bellies.

> Old pirates, yes, they rob I,
> Sold I to the merchant ships
> Minutes after they took I
> From the bottomless pit
> But my 'and was made strong
> By the 'and of the Almighty
> We forward in this generation
> Triumphantly
> Won't you help to sing
> These songs of freedom?
> 'Cause all I ever have
> Redemption songs
> Redemption songs
>
> Emancipate yourself from mental slavery
> None but our self can free our minds
> Have no fear for atomic energy
> 'Cause none of them can stop the time
> How long shall dey kill our prophets
> While we stand aside and look?
> Some say it's just a part of it
> We've got to fulfil de book
> Won't you help to sing
> These songs of freedom?
> 'Cause all I ever have
> Redemption songs. (Repeat)
>
> (Bob Marley, 'Redemption Song', 1980)

(Each woman sings as though the words were keys to releasing the angst they carry deep within. As they get to the second verse, release is evident. The voices are strong and harmonised. Some faces are contorted, others with widened smiles. There is no evidence of self-consciousness and those crying make no attempt to conceal the tears. At the end of the music, a couple of the women ring out the chorus a cappella style.)

> Emancipate yourself from mental slavery
> None, but our self can free our minds
> Have no fear for atomic energy
> 'Cause none of them can stop the time
> How long shall dey kill our prophets
> While we stand aside and look?
> Some say it's just a part of it
> We've got to fulfil de book
>
> Won't you help to sing
> These songs of freedom?
> 'Cause all I ever had
> Redemption songs
> All I ever had
> Redemption songs
> These songs of freedom
> Songs of freedom.

At the end of the rendition there is silence. The silence is soon high jacked by sounds of deep breathing and a few laboured sighs. Almost in reverence, each woman closes her eyes.

Mama B walks forward and grasps the hand of Sankofa, Sankofa takes hold of GyeNyame's hand and within seconds all the hands in the room are linked. Then, Aya, one of the quieter members of the group begins to chant the line ...

Aya: emancipate yourself from mental slavery, none but ourselves can free our minds emancipate yourself from mental slavery, none but ourselves can free our minds.

Her words echo through the large room. Then each woman in unison repeats the line. Before long there is an explosion of disjointed voices chanting,

> None but ourselves can free our minds.

Bittersweet realisation – hope we are the last

Some of the women walk to the peripheries of the room. Most seeking personal space within 'the space', when they find their space, they stand, in silence. In time, each woman returns to her seat, there is no embarrassment, no awkwardness, just an unspoken knowing.

Mama B: (Stepping forward.) 'Well, ladies, ethics would say, that right now I should consider your support needs, I mean that was (the capital letters that follow indicate a raised voice) POWER-FUL ... SO MUCH EMOTION ... I would be admonished to signpost you to counselling or something. So, to keep in line with ethical considerations ... come and talk to me afterwards, if you need to speak about what just happened, okay.'

There was an outburst of laughter. Emerging from amidst the laughter is GyeNyame's voice:

GyeNyame: 'Mama B, tell the ethics people that they are often part of our problem, what we just experienced in this space is the kind of "support therapy" we need.

All we need is space to explore our way ... using the insights of those who understood us and our struggle, like prophet and philosopher Robert Nesta Marley. Right here, just now, as well as other times on this journey, "we have just been". We, without having to analyse or vocalise, understood the tears and the silence. We have an empathetic association with both as well as with each other as sojourners.'

Mama B: (Smiling.) 'Okay GyeNyame, we hear you! In academic terms, we just positioned ourselves between ontology and epistemology. Simply because we are free to be! We have had the time and space to reflect as well as the group association. These are the elements that create the right environment for us to grow and develop. It was Lorde (2007) who said: "The white fathers told us: I think, therefore I am. The Black mother within each of us ... whispers in our dreams: I feel; therefore, I can be free" (p. 38). I think that's what you're saying GyeNyame. We felt what the late, great Bob Marley spoke to us through his lyrics. When we sing, emancipate yourself from mental slavery, in this context, it means the same as the academics would say, decolonising the mind. We relate to the "mental slavery," don't we? The words hit our understanding. Our parents would say, "feels it, knows it" ... We share a history of mental enslavement, because of the partial education meted out to us to ensure we consistently occupy subordinate spaces.

Sankofa: But we are taking responsibility by creating spaces to liberate and educate ourselves.'

(Interrupts.) 'Yeah, let's put some flesh on theory, for me theory has very little to teach me until I add human experience to it. In my experience, too many of our mature Black nurses describe themselves as "good bedside nurses". I have no doubt that they are, but what this journey has forced me to look at is the root of descriptions or "labels". When the "label" good bedside side nurse was first introduced it was an implication by the Colonial British nurses that the Black nurses' knowledge would only ever be "practical", never "intellectual". Therefore, Black nurses would never be able to be managers or leaders. Now, whenever a Black nurse uses the "good bedside nurse" label I often feel that they are resigning themselves to the subordinated position they have been apportioned.

Now I challenge every nurse that uses that limiting label. I've said to Black nurses, go read about the history of nursing and then you may want to further develop that thought, for example, I'm not only a good bedside nurse but I also possess the skills, knowledge and aspiration to ... inviting them to finish the sentence based on the conversation we were having, for example, be an excellent manager or an outstanding matron.'

Mama B: 'Sankofa, living up to her name which means go back into the past to learn from it so you can inform the future. Thanks for putting the flesh on theory. Okay, ladies, some of you have emailed Sankofa and me to share your frustrations with what you describe as a lack of closure in our "spaces" sometimes. You have shared your views that the sessions are not long enough and that we need to make them longer. Well, though we have responded to your emails, Sankofa and I felt your concerns need to be addressed here too.

Firstly, we agree that there hasn't been a structured approach to wrapping up the sessions and we will try to address that today. We do think however, that part of the problem is that the sessions have been a lot longer than we had planned and that has often been driven by our desires to share more. We've done this in agreement with you, but it's important that we remind ourselves of a few things. We will never have complete answers to any of the issues we are exploring in these spaces. Remember the messiness discussion we had in our earlier sessions? There's no sat nav, no A–Z, no bible. We are doing something that may have been done by others with similar aims ... but never by us.

Secondly, there will never be sufficient time. Sankofa and I have tried to put a skeleton themed programme together and it was our hope that in discussion, and with agreement, we would flesh it out with you and my word has that been done ... but in fleshing out ... and going with a revised, agreed plan, we have sometimes lost our focus on managing time. I must say however, there is no denying that much learning has happened in the space. But our learning has been experimental. A pilot if you please! It is inevitable that it feels unpolished and unfinished and we will never have enough time to get everything in. What we are trying to expose in a couple of sessions would take researchers in the academy years, this should be a longitudinal study, sorry ... a study done over several years.

So, co-seekers, what excites us is the fact that we have been ignited, we are engaging with text and authors and YOU are contributing to the process of making sense of OUR educational journeys of this time. So, can we throw out a challenge? Can we accept the messiness as an important part of the journey? Can we live with the lack of closure sometimes? The incompleteness? And our biggest challenge ... can we continue this work in lots of other spaces when this group ceases to be; sharing the lessons we have learned from it? Can we? Ladies, can you? One of the things we've loved about your emails was that you were not merely complaining but you were coming up with suggestions for solutions ... Now I'll hand over to Sankofa. Oops, before I hand over, any questions?'

(There was no verbal response, just shaking of heads and smiles.)

Sankofa: 'Thanks, Mama B, and thanks, ladies. I incubated the idea of "the space" in isolation. I didn't have the faith to think that we could really make it happen. I dreamt it ... I desired it and longed for it ... but I must confess that I doubted whether busy women, who had been stung by education would want to fully engage. But you have, and your insights and contributions have been a real boost to my resolution. That said, when I received Bese Saka's email suggesting that to save time you were going to create posters outlining the summaries of your pitfalls and roadblocks, I danced and danced with joy! Picture me doing an African jig around my living room screeching ... we've got a vision and it's alive ... it's alive ...'

GyeNyame: (With a wry smile – interrupts.) 'Our imagination isn't that great Sankofa, can we have a visual demonstration, please?'

(The women laugh, Sankofa leaves space for the laughter, then continues.)

Sankofa: 'I'll save it for another time GyeNyame, the routine needs perfecting ... and I need a dancing partner so when we're done today, I'll get you to help me perfect my moves and we'll perform together for the others ... Anyway, you trouble maker ... let's move on. I know that you have brought along your posters. Would you put them on the walls so we can all have a look and remind ourselves of the themes? I've got Blu-Tack here for you.'

GyeNyame: (Voice broken.) 'Can I just add something Sankofa, please?'

Sankofa: 'Yeah, go ahead, GyeNyame.'

GyeNyame: 'I thought about whether I was going to talk about this ... as you can probably tell from the tremor in my voice, this still hurts really badly ... I didn't put it on the poster, now I wish I had. One of the most deepening wounds from the breakdown in communication between the university and workplace for me was ... getting letters from bailiffs to my home ...

(She breaks downs and sobs, Akoben goes to stand with her.)

I need to say this ... excuse me ... (She uses breathing techniques to compose herself.) My otherwise extremely supportive husband was so mad when on more than one occasion we got letters from bailiffs for the non-payment of the university fees. I lost count of the number of calls I made to the Trust's learning and development department but for two years the issue was unresolved ... I passed all my assignments, I paid a tutor to help me to prepare for the anatomy and physiology exam as I am a dyslexic learner and had failed the first two attempts because I ran out of time. I passed the third only because I paid for extra tuition. I turned up to deliver my final presentation, yes you heard correctly, my final presentation. I was stopped at the door and turned away like a person who had no right to be on the premises. Despite my pleading, my calls to the Trust to prove I wasn't liable for the fees and my tears, I was sent home ... I was not allowed to present. I was fully prepared but the university said my fees were not paid by the Trust. That was it, this wasn't the first time ... It was so humiliating, I vowed never to return to that campus.' (Tears streaming down her face ... GyeNyame gets up and leaves the room. Sankofa signals the women to continue whilst she goes after GyeNyame.)

(The women put up their posters, then everyone moves around the room reading each other's contributions.)

Bittersweet realisation – hope we are the last

Nsoromma - Pits / Shits and Survivor

Lecturers: a couple of lecturers were alright, but others just did not want to know. The lectures were okay. But assignments and booklets, it's the wording in there I had difficulty and got frustrated with! I'd tell the lecturers that I didn't understand and they'd repeat themselves. I wanted to say, I'm not hard of hearing, I heard you, but I don't get it!

I OFTEN wondered, why can't they find DIFFERENT WAY to explain it to me?

I had a mentor and an assessor on the ward but my mentor went on maternity leave so I was getting shipped around to different mentors. Because they said it was a work based course, I expected to have more responsibility at work, but there was no structure. I took on a few extra tasks like bloods and cannulations. All other tasks I was doing before I started the course.

Exams are not my thing... this was a work-based course, yet it was the exam that ended it for me. When will universities learn that exams aren't for everyone?

NO ONE considered ME or was willing to HEAR ME. I'm not being funny, but to me it felt like looking at my colour and my background and saying in my words... 'nah sod ya'! No one gave a shit about you!

But then there's another thing they tell all us if you apply for the foundation degree 'oh yes you can get a job out of it'. I've got somebody on my ward who has been finished for years and she's t still waiting to get a job.

I'm hopeful, I survived, I'm okay in myself. I just feel so tired and drained, I don't think I've got anywhere, but something new will come to me. I just need to find a new path.

Figure 1. Nsoromma – Banking model of education.

NSAA - SELF SUSTAINED

Mentor: I used my mentor to sign off my course books. I found my own support system. I pulled on another Black woman (an independent friend) for peer support. We had a great friendship, we could chat loads about different things in life and everything… but even with her I found that she hadn't really got the enthusiasm… the drive wasn't there… so though we would meet up to work, we lacked discipline and identified it.**I took on the job to keep us focussed.**

We were told that on completion of the fd, we would only have to do 18 months of nursing. That turned out to be untrue! In reality, those who wanted to go on to do nursing, found that the fd did not exempt you from any part of the nursing course.

Lectures were okay, nothing special! If I didn't get something, I spoke to my peer or my daughter.

From the beginning of the second year, I was just wanting to just finish the course… **it just took my life away**. I had this beautiful home and I weren't enjoying it… my kids… I needed to be with my kids more and not in libraries or on campus.

Personally, **completing the course has been an achievement!** I've got my picture up with my gown on. It is a great personal achievement. I know my dad was very proud when I gave him my photo. My mum said… well done girl and you know… I feel good… my kids feel good…that I've done it…

There has been no economic advantage. I can honestly say getting a fd has not really impacted my work much either.
Though I'm proud to have finished, I don't judge those who count the cost of going to university and wonder if it's worth it!

Figure 2. NSAA – Education and work did not uplift me.

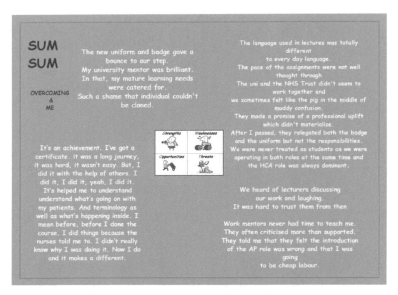

Figure 3. Sumsum – No affective education.

Figure 4. GyeNyame – Education that oppresses.

Bittersweet realisation – hope we are the last

Bese Saka
Barriers, Pitfalls and Personal lessons

Biggest challenge was trying to get support. Seriously, it was trying to get support and battling on through more or less on my own. Getting through it with lack of support.

Study time, you wasn't getting it. My mentor, always too busy.. I'm like, you are supposed to be my mentor, where's the encouragement? So at Uni, told the personal tutor and stuff.

The university offered my placement mentor a mentoring course. Yeah, cause I told them, she doesn't know what she's doing.

Mentor, I didn't even see my one. The second year, I never worked with her once. Well, I worked with her on the same shift, but we never did anything together.

I said to my manager, I said, I'm going to need time to study because the mornings,used to be quiet then, she said that Wednesday would be a good day but, then she put me on clinic when all the other staff were chatting, sitting around doing cleaning.

When I was doing the course it was like, oh yea, there'll be a job because we haven't got any APs here and it would be good for the department .And then it's the second year and like you're asking in your PDRs what's happening am I gonna get it? And it's like, oh I don't know financial situation

Reverting to a band 2 uniform after 2 years working as a band 4 in training.

I feel bleep, bleep, bleep. I don't cuss so I say bleep, bleep, bleep. Two years of struggle, hard work, built up my skills... what really got me angry is when the manager turned round and said: " but if you don't get your band 4 and you go back to a band 2, will you still do the clinics that need the AP skills?" 'cause you'll have to keep your skills current!

It's made me stronger and I... I ask questions more. You know like before, now I don't mind asking oh what's that, or do you mind if I come in and watch ? I'm more like wanna see more and you know it's built up my... confidence to ask more. Made me tougher.

Figure 5. Bese Saka – Educated to regress.

Akoma

Lectures and Essays:
Too long - not well paced, too much reliance on powerpoint and far too many handouts

Assignment briefs - Too wordy with unnecessarily complex language

Me:
To be honest, I don't think I've failed, I say my circumstances where why I didn't complete the course. I wouldn't class myself as a failure.

Programme:
Not enough joined up thinking, too heavy on theory, too little practical. The university and workplace worked totally separately which made life difficult for the students.

Figure 6. Aroma – Rethinking educational failure.

Aya
– I know myself and how I got here!

Yeah! I'm happy now...I'm more motivated now, before I did this course I had no status. I was just here serving tea...every time, I was just serving food. I often thought, I'm a Healthcare Assistant, why can't the nurse give me some other tasks to do.

I overcame the hurdles of an unstructured course with boring lectures and tutors who didn't seem to expect much from me. I was supported by a black student nurse. She was bright, ambitious and even when she was fed up with me, I just kept going to work alongside her. She was brilliant, she was my private mentor.

I was promised a band 4 position, it's been SIX years and I still haven't got it. I am constantly asked to use the skills I gained on the course, but I don't get paid for it.

My manager insulted me the first time I asked about the new position, when I asked her the third time, she accused me of harassing her.

But I rise each shift to serve my patients.

Figure 7. Aya – Education uplifts self esteem.

MATIE MASIE - POTHOLES, HURDLES & ME.

Mentor at work... I didn't have one, I was doing everything myself really. I was appointed one, but she had her own issues and we never got together to put in a plan.

When I moved wards, I was given, R and I don't think she was that interested in being my mentor... I felt it was because I wasn't a student nurse, they paid more interest in the student nurses.

Lectures: sometimes when you can't understand something and when you ask the questions it's as if tutors are too busy to answer, or help you... the funny thing about it is sometimes they'd say, if you need any help you must come to us. But when you do go to them everyone is always too busy.

I tried at first but after that I didn't bother because I'm thinking you know what, why bother, because no one is gonna bother with me anyway.

The Library, I hadn't been in education for ages. I didn't have a library induction. I just followed the other girls. Then I had a library fine because I forgot to bring books back..my fine was about three hours pay. I stopped going to the library because I couldn't afford to keep paying... And then you couldn't afford to keep buying the books either.

I'm not that good on the computer... so I didn't really like the computer, but I did want to have better skills. I'm just...a one finger typist and you didn't just have to do your class work, you had to use moodle...

Staff were confused asking, what is the fd? And then they would say things like, oh it's just like the SENs that they use to have years ago... things like that...And it's like some people were probably threatened as well, so that's why they didn't wanna help me...

I just tried to do my own thing... but it didn't help, because with a course like that you need somebody behind you to motivate and help you.
The qualified did not help me. But when they wanted help, they'd say, " Matie you should be able to do the bloods now" You've been on that course haven't you? The way I saw it they wanted somebody to be cheap labour... that's the way I saw it... it's still happening now...

For me, I honestly feel I've wasted time. I'm disappointed.

You know I just wanted to... I just wanted to do achieve as a black person.
You know because here, they always say that... you know... that we can't... we're always treated different to everybody else... We're always treated as though we are a lower class... I've overheard people say it...so maybe I'm a little bitter.

Figure 8. Matie Masie – Time poor education doesn't work.

Bittersweet realisation – hope we are the last 95

Dame Dame - Hurdles present to be jumped over!

MENTOR:

The mentors are willing to teach the student nurses they didn't seem to see us as students. They didn't really value or recognise our trainee role in the team us as part of the team. Student nurses got more attention, on a number of occasions, I had to remind my mentor that I'm your student as well.

It really took a long time and a lot of complaining to finally get some shifts where my mentor and I could actually work together. We were rarely on the same shift. In fact, I sometimes had to come into work on my off duty so I could develop the clinical skills and complete my workbooks.

PROGRAMME:

Not many of the modules on the programme were linked to the workplace / clinical skills

As an assistant practitioner I am expected to like have my own patients delegated by the nurse and working under her supervision to meet their care needs, with the exception of medication. That is NOT happening.

I've lost TRUST in the organisation!

When I was doing the course I had a badge which said, 'Trainee Assistant Practitioner'. Now I've qualified as an Assistant Practitioner, the nurses use me in the role because I ask to do things. I don't want to lose my skills.

YET I NOW WEAR A BADGE THAT SAYS Healthcare Assistant

I was promised a band 4 position on completion, since completing I've been to the matron and who says there is no funding. I asked whether funding could be sought to up upgrade me to a band three, she said NO!

THE ONLY CONVERSATION I HAVE HAD WITH THE ORGANISATION WAS TO BE TOLD BY MY MANAGER, YOU NEED TO STOP WEARING THE TRAINEE UNIFORM BECAUSE YOU ARE A BAND TWO.

Completing the course has changed how I work as nurses now see me as being more competent to do other clinical. Things that they would be doing themselves, I am now allocated to do.

Figure 9. Dame Dame – We were not given student status.

AKOBEN - HOW I WADED THROUGH CRAP BUT CAME UP SMELLING OF ROSES

The lectures: We ALL complained about teaching skills, in too many instances they were non existent we had presentations just read to us. I don't know why they badda right, 'cause we can read for weself...

I found it quite insulting... I remember saying to one lecturer... I'm not being rude but you're just reading what's on the presentation... you're not telling me nothing. I said I can look at the powerpoint at home. I said you need to explain to me, because you're giving me this assignment and I can't get my head around it. When people would ask her something, she goes. "Well, I don't know the medical jargon". I would say, I'm not asking you for the medical jargon... just tell me how dis fi flow through dat...and open up... you know... I need the nitty-gritty... and you know... it was just like she couldn't comprehend what we were on about...and her teaching... her style was just so crap.

It wasn't all bad though, THERE WAS ONE EXCEPTION

He'd say something like say... you had a bowl... you had a piece of cloth...and you put water in it...and you put this powder in it...and it filters through... He'd just simplify things so that you could actually see it in your head... whereas if you said to others can you explain that another way because I don't understand... they couldn't find another example to give you... so you were still left stupid. I remember the good one was was explaining to us...and half of us didn't understand what the hell the tutor talking about...and they simplified it to the point of talking about traffic lights and there was...OH... from most of us in the room, cause we all got it then! Most lecturers would stand up in front of the class... presentation...der...der...der...der...der...der... ok, and if you have any problems you can email me...I don't wanna email ya... I wanna talk to ya...

I think we were meant to start in May...Clear inna July... we still no start de course...'cause the tutor was off sick...

My manager appointed me a work place mentor, now I would not mind that she gave me X... if me and X talked... but we don't even flipping talk. The woman was so lazy she was one of those trained nurses who did not want students. She didn't want to have any body under her wings to train and show the ropes....I remember... this mentor was leaving. I went to the new manager... I said, how is this going to work for me... X is going and I need a new mentor. I had a new manager by then, the new manager goes how did you get X as your mentor? I said... your predecessor gave her to me. She asked, what did you do to upset my predecessor? I CHOSE MY NEW MENTOR AND OUR RELATIONSHIP IS FANTASTIC - My choice is a BRILLIANT TRAINER.

Going to university was an up hill struggle... I do not think that going to uni will ever be easy for anybody... if it was easy... we would all do it...

Nurses were very negative in their comments and approach to me when I started this course...very negative...
I never left the HCA role, I was a HCA/TAP

I know that I am not going to get that light blue uniform that the APs have now... cause they can't give me job... that's fine...as long as they don't hold me back... it's kinda bitter / sweet because I don't want them to stop me using the skills I've learned, but I also know I won't get paid for those skills.

Figure 10. Akoben – Education struggle and breakthrough.

(Following the readings, the women naturally gravitate to those accounts they resonate with most and start re-sharing. There is much chatter and filling in of gaps as they retell. The conversations are choreographed with a range of gesticulations.)

(After approximately fifteen minutes Akoben stops the group and suggests that the point they have just been discussing privately is worth sharing publicly.)

Akoben: 'Can I add something we just spoke about but we didn't include on our posters, I think it is important. The whole uniform and name badge occurrences really confused our patients. Those of us who undertake AP roles in our HCA uniforms are often looked on suspiciously by patients and their relatives. We find ourselves having to justify and explain that we are qualified to undertake clinical duties delegated to us.'

Mama B: 'That addition is very important, Akoben. I hope those incidents were communicated to matrons, as patients need to trust that staff are competent and a quick way of doing so is by taking notice of uniforms and name badges. Ladies, can we finish off our conversations and come back together please? I suggest we have a comfort break of fifteen minutes, then I will introduce our speaker. Fifteen minutes then, ladies.'

(The women disperse in a range of directions. They quickly return to their seats expectantly.)

Mama B: 'Well, thank you for coming back early. It is my pleasure to welcome Dr Owo Adobe. Dr Adobe has been a life-long friend of mine and she has asked me not to do the formal academic introduction. In fact, in our discussion about her joining us today, she asked if the format could be more conversational rather than a lecture. I took the liberty of saying that would be okay, but you said you would prefer a formal talk so ladies I now present to you Dr Owo Adobe.'

Dr Owo Adobe: 'Well, good evening sisters. I can't tell you how pleased I am to be here. When Mama B told me about your gathering, I felt a spiritual connection with what you were doing. Each time we spoke I enquired of you and was heartened when I heard that you were still going. From small acorns, mighty oaks grow. Do not underestimate what you are doing here because of the size of the group or your perceived lack of experience. I wish to affirm you.

From your posters, it is evident that in-spite of poor mentoring, you endured. In-spite of lectures that neither ignited, enlightened or transformed you, you endured. Whether you wore a TAP uniform or were professionally relegated to your previously held HCA uniform and position, you endured. Even when the university and workplace systems worked to disable and disempower you, you endured. Be assured of this fact, whoever we are, to succeed, we must endure.

I just want to say, Mama B, was showing me professional respect when she used my title. But I am Owo. No need for titles here! I can honestly say that when I heard about some of the conversations you have been having, I was really looking forward to joining you. When the invitation came, I was looking forward to the dialogue. So, needless to say, I am a little disappointed that my brief is to do a formal talk. Nevertheless, I will try my best to sow some seedlings in the epistemological soil you have been tilling and hopefully, even in my absence through your nurturing they will develop and grow. To begin, I'll acknowledge one of the pioneers of post-colonial thinking, the one whose name this theatre bears, philosopher and psychologist, Frantz Fanon. Of education under colonialism Fanon (1967) said:

> Intellectual alienation is a creation of middle-class society. What I call middle-class society is any society that becomes rigidified in predetermined forms, forbidding all evolution, all gains, all progress, all discovery. I call middle-class a closed society in which ... ideas and men are corrupt. (p. 224)

Fanon's view was one that was supported by revolutionary educationalists, like Freire. Apple (2013) articulates Freire's views stating:

> The dominant class, deaf to the need for a critical reading of the world, insists on the purely technical training of the working class, training with which that class should reproduce itself as such. Progressive ideology, however, cannot separate technical training from political preparation, just as it cannot separate the practise of reading the word from reading discourse. (p. 28)

Now I understand that in your context, class is not considered to be amongst the dominant considerations for you. However, not now, but maybe in phase two of your journeys you may consider how the hegemonic community view class and control. I fully understand that this is an epistemological trajectory, this is about you. However, in any battle, knowing your opponent's views, strategies and plans results in you being a stronger opponent.

What I surmise from your recordings, as well as the accounts of several adult mature first-generation university students, is that you were not exposed to an education which challenged or stimulated you to think critically or otherwise. Educators then need to revisit the question: What is the purpose of education? Are universities and workplaces working towards ensuring that the educational experience is not only a positive but a productive one for all students? Unfortunately, your experiences suggest that HE is an unnecessarily treacherous place to navigate. Apple (2013) argues the following of education in general, but I think this argument is also very true for work-based education. "Education is seen as simply factories producing test scores and docile workers" (p. 4). He further asserts that our education systems generally focus on "production and consumption" and what is often missing is a consideration of those hurt by this approach.

GyeNyame's poster jumped out at me, she is one who has been hurt by the "systems" she tried to navigate in pursuit of personal and professional development. I felt your distress, you articulated yourself well in that poster. It is incredibly frustrating when processes that should be established and routine consistently fail. Such an ignominy! But I encourage you, my sister, my friend, do not stop dreaming! Like Maya Angelou's poem asserts, find your own way to "still rise". You may have been denied a positive educational experience, pay increase, promotion, but you do not have to accept the imposition of failure. Your identity is not fixed, it is fluid, therefore, you may be down but keep engaging in spaces such as this one because your voice has very much been a dominant one. Keep rising! Don't rule out returning to university either.

When we sang "Redemption Song" at the point of repetition, I was reminding myself that I needed to constantly work against the concept that because of my race and gender I had to restrict myself to peripheral spaces. I wonder what would happen if we were all involved in a process of consistently emancipating ourselves from the enslaved thoughts of being "frauds" in spaces because we are obviously a minority. We so often believe that "failure" makes us "failures" instead of acknowledging that oftentimes the disappointments and heartaches create and provide opportunities for us to learn, to think differently, to be creative and potentially to find

Bittersweet realisation – hope we are the last 99

our own, culturally appropriate solutions. George Sefa Dei (2010) reminds us that Fanon was:

> instrumental in shaping and refining the thought that colonisation is equally about a study of subjectivity and power relations. Colonialism and colonisation had significant effects on the psyche of the colonised. (p. 11)

I recall earlier on in my career addressing issues around the internalisation of a limited view of my skills and abilities. You have been able to explore how a colonial approach to nursing education resulted in the partial skilling of Caribbean nurses. We learnt that the scientific aspects of nursing was not part of the syllabus for Black nurses in the Caribbean until they took responsibility for designing and delivering the nursing syllabus which would enlighten and propel them into the professional spaces they wished to inhabit!

In this space, you are committed to what Fanon (1967) described as the "two-sided-ness" approach to the theorising of colonisation. Dubios (1973), Sefa Dei (2010) and others argue that to critically engage with issues of domination and oppression, with a view to "dismantling" the practices of oppression, both the oppressors and the oppressed need to be studied. In both groups, the strategies of resistance need to be considered. In this space, you are making your attempt and I applaud you. As I reflect on your posters, the words of West (1998) came back to me, he claims:

> The Black experience offers philosophy a profound sense of the tragic and the comic rooted in heroic efforts to preserve human dignity ... in short, a deep blues' sensibility that highlights concrete existence, history, struggle, lived experiences and joy. (p. 39)

Your posters included all that West alluded to; aligning West's quote to what's happening in this space excites me. I can't tell you how much. You see, here, you are pursing your own philosophy, you are engaging with and thrashing ideas that will enable you and others to better comprehend the education you experienced as you all move forward. For so long, we, as Yancy (1998) suggests: "have allowed the white philosopher to be the sole definer of our reality" (p. 9). Therein lay a great deal of our problems. I wonder if there have been studies that have explored how many "researched groups" access the research findings their lived experiences informed? Freire (in Apple, 2013) asserts: "we must develop and present our counter hegemonic perspectives as a way of interrupting colonial dominance in education and in cultural studies in general" (p. 35). That's what's happening in this space.

What is also imperative as we interrupt the hegemonic approaches is that we are explicit about our bias. As we share our stories, we declare, we do not wish to be objective.

It was Fanon who argued that it would be both "impossible and dishonest" for us to claim objectivity. As "self" researchers, culture is an important consideration of our viewing of the world. However, in most cases, culture from a place of "knowing" is not fully explored, especially when "we are researched" by those who have historically and currently position us as "other" in education and employment. Often what Caucasian researchers fail to fully understand is ... actually, I will use the words of Fanon (1967) who articulates this thought much better than I could. Fanon asserts that during colonisation:

> The inferior complex was created by the death and burial of local cultures. (p. 18)

He further argues, and we all know this through our lived experiences, that Blacks have dual dimensions. We are very much aware that in so many aspects of our lives we behave differently amongst Caucasians than we do amongst our fellow Blacks. I can also tell you from my lived experience that Caucasians who are advocates of equality, social justice and "engaged" pedagogy are generally as enslaved by the HE and work-based institutions as we are. I'll borrow West's (1998) assertion here:

> This philosophical journey is mediated by value laden interpretations of the Black woman's struggle for equality and freedom; the major bias of this inquiry is the desire for freedom and equality. (p. 23)

We are making our bias explicit, that's what this approach requires of us.

I'll draw on the psychological expertise of Fanon who stated,

> The "negro" is enslaved by his inferiority, the white man enslaved by his superiority alike behave in accordance with a neurotic orientation. (p. 60)

He follows on to say, "negroes" inferiority complex is particularly intensified among the most educated'. I would add here, amongst those "we assume are educated". Think about your working context where you are placed in bands for your pay. I assume that as you predominantly reside and are kept in residence in the lower tiers of the banding structure you must invest in self-awareness and self-esteem to co-inhabit the working space as people worthy of respect.

I generally find myself, more often than I would like, in professional spaces where I am the only minority. However, I am learning that I am responsible for my projection in those spaces. After all, it was Fanon (1967) again who said that:

> A white man in a colony has never felt inferior in any respect ... the colonial, even though he is "in the minority" does not feel that this makes him inferior. (p. 92)

So, let's ask ourselves, who the hell has the right to keep us inferior and what the hell do WE need to do to correct the maligned position? I will close this section with a final thought on breaking the colonial mindset from Lorde (2007) who asserted:

> Those of us who are poor, who are lesbians, who are blacks, who are older – know that survival is not an academic skill. It is learning how to stand alone, unpopular and sometimes reviled, and how to make common cause with those others identified as outside the structures in order to define and seek a world in which we can flourish. It is learning how to take our differences and make them strengths. For the masters' tools will never dismantle the masters' house. (p. 112)

There is a quote conceived out of experiential pain, if ever we've heard one! Moving on I must say I am perturbed by the way the institution uses their power to control your professional identities. Your recall provided me with insights that made me question the psychological impact your journey must have had on you.

I understand that professionally, you were uplifted, through mediums that both colleagues and service users understood. You were provided with new uniforms and name badges. Some of you shared the professional pride the epaulets provided whilst accepting that they also created some angst within teams, as seniors didn't always understand what your uniform represented. What I consider to be an ethical violation was the fact that for some of you, even after successfully completing the fd were told to stop wearing the uniform and the name badge, but still asked to perform tasks linked to the newly qualified role. How unjust! How could an institution that "claims to care and provide care" do that to their staff and colleagues? Who sanctions such actions?

It's an interesting observation that when abuses, such as Stafford hospital, are publicised, politicians, the public and decent human beings demand investigations, accountability and change. I accept that lives were lost at Stafford, so it's right that investigations should be undertaken and reports and recommendations made.

However, we fail to consider the fact that we annihilate people professionally and psychologically. Who gives a damn?

I don't suppose I will ever be able to approach a hospital again without asking, where does the balance lie in this institution between the number of people they make well and the numbers they make sick through their practices and surreptitious conducts? I will also be wondering how many professional terminations it undertakes as it strives to keep its "peaks snowy" and managers and leaders comfortable. I understand that cost efficiencies have resulted in "down banding" in some areas of the health service. However, it is an absurd concept that you can gain a qualification then have your uniform and name badge "relegated" but required to take on additional tasks in line with the qualification.

I'm sorry ladies, but at this point, my blood boils ... widening participation may have appeared to partially open doors, but what seems invisible to too many on the inside is the barbed wired fences of injustice that must be navigated to stay in and succeed. I respect your resilience. Your aspiration to become "recognised professionals", has left you fatigued, exposed and vulnerable. You have had your professional accomplishments stripped off, by the so-called powers that be.

By no means am I saying that you should view yourselves solely as victims. I wish to echo the view of Baldwin (1985) here. He asserts:

> I refuse absolutely to speak from the point of view of the victim. The victim can have no point of view for precisely so long as he thinks of himself as a victim. The testimony of the victim corroborates the chains that binds him and ... consoles the jailer. (p. 78)

Our message is, hello ... we see what you've done ... we understand it, we're broken but not dead. Disappointed? Yes! Bloody

Bittersweet realisation – hope we are the last 103

angry and annoyed? Yes, both with you and ourselves. Had we known our history, you would not have duped us, using the same strategies you used to dupe our parents. So, we are as mad with ourselves as we are with you. That's why this space and this approach is necessary. We need to get the word out! We must get the word out!

I'll end this section by paraphrasing a thought of Freire (1994) widening participation has placed a "dark cloud" over us because it "reduced education to mere training" and annihilated our dreams. But whilst there is life, there is hope ... still we rise, tentatively, but we rise. The lovely thing about the audience here is that I can ignore the stuffy formalities. I'll stop there and suggest we have a comfort break?'

(The women disperse. Owo consults with Mama B, who suggests she goes ahead with the practical activity they previously discussed. The women return.)

Mama B: 'Okay, ladies, thanks for returning on time. Owo is asking your permission to change the format to a discussion. Would that be okay?'

Akoben: 'Yeah, see, here is a lecturer who knows that she needs to break things up and get us involved. Another reason I love this space!'

Owo: 'Ladies, I would like to encourage you to break into three groups and we'll have twenty minutes to discuss the following.

(She turns the flip-chart around revealing the task.)

Following your fd experience, you are asked to convey messages or ask questions to the following:

The university
The funders of your course
The NHS Trust – your workplace

I will give you flipchart paper and pens and you can be as creative as you like in your expressions. At the end of the twenty minutes, your groups will merge and you will be given a further ten minutes to consolidate your messages. Finally, you will be asked to add a message to a mature Black woman who is considering taking up a work-based WP opportunity. At the end, you will agree and decide how to share just the key messages. Any questions?'

(The women disperse without acknowledging Owo's question. The time elapses and the group nominates Akoben to feedback.)

Akoben: 'First, I've got to say that the groups shared how difficult this was. It was harder than we had anticipated. We added a section we called messages to self and here we use quotes that we have had read, recorded and memorised as part of this journey, quotes that remind us to stay united:

Messages to ourselves:
One finger cannot pick up something from the ground
One hand cannot by itself lift a load off the head
One leg cannot run
One head cannot form a committee

To become a force to be reckoned with, we must abandon mistrust amongst ourselves and unite. I'll shout this message to our sisters. Black women we want to gather with intentional solidarity so we can articulate our frustrations with inequalities and through our interconnectedness journey to our self-defined, political, professional and personal identities.

Finally, and this is one worth remembering: Drum roll please ...
"You never
  hit
    a
      person
        over
          the
            head
              when
                you
                  have
                    your
                      finger
                        in
                        their mouth."

Bittersweet realisation – hope we are the last

The room erupts with laughter.

Gye-Nyame:	'Yeah, love it. Let's stop expecting those who malign and oppress us to find solutions for us. We need to be instigators of our own liberations. Now, Mama B, Sankofa and Owo we would like to convey our messages using an adaptation of the traditional African call and response.'
Owo:	'L-o-v-i-n-g i-t! So, your first message is to the funders ... let's have it!'
GyeNyame:	'We wanted WP equality not the poisoned chalice of opportunity!'
Akoben:	'How did you hold the NHS Trust and HEI accountable for the funds invested? Did you request formative and summative evaluations of the programmes and how were these used?'
GyeNyame:	'We wanted WP equality not the poisoned chalice of opportunity!'
Akoben:	'How were we to inform you that our "opportunities" resulted in: A poor educational experience? An unfulfilled promise of salary uplift? An unfulfilled promise to patients that the NHS would be better staffed?'
GyeNyame:	'We wanted WP equality not the poisoned chalice of opportunity!'
Akoben:	'Why weren't our experiences and expectations part of your evaluation? What responsibility will you take for the fd "travesty"?'
GyeNyame:	'Now Dame-Dame and SunSum, it's over to you with questions/messages for the university.'
Dame-Dame:	'We longed for transformative pedagogy, not a colonised approach to study!'
SunSum:	'Why do you limit your teaching methods to talks and powerpoints? Why did you resist us when we asked that you link theory to practice?'
Dame-Dame:	'We longed for transformative pedagogy, not a colonised approach to study!'
SunSum:	'What stopped you trying to get to know us? Let's talk about why your learning environments were not conducive to our learning? What else could we have done to convince you that we longed for you to demonstrate that you believed in us?'
Dame-Dame:	'We longed for transformative pedagogy, not a colonised approach to study!'
SunSum:	'Why did you allow the issue of funding to impede our educational experience though you partnered with our workplace? Talk to us about how important full inductions are to mature students' survival in a HEI.

Why does your HEI have so few tutors that we felt we could relate to?'

The caller and responder for the messages to the workplace will be Nsoramma and Nsaa.

Nsoramma: 'Your rhetoric and our lived experiences are worlds apart, have the courage to challenge institutional discrimination!'

Nsaa: 'Can we discuss how not giving us student status, sent a message to colleagues at work that they could berate us?

Can we explore the fact that because we had no professional identity, our educational experience lacked quality?'

Nsoramma: 'Your rhetoric and our lived experiences are worlds apart, have the courage to challenge institutional discrimination!'

Nsaa: 'Can we be enlightened on why you considered it acceptable to promise salary upgrade but failed to honour your promise?

What should be your responsibility for the fact that some of us were ejected from our course because you failed to pay our fees on time?'

Nsoramma: 'Your rhetoric and our lived experiences are worlds apart, have the courage to challenge institutional discrimination!'

Nsaa: 'Mentors didn't engage but why should they when there was no consequence for not engaging? Why did you not take an interest in our experience? In the beginning, you shovelled the "support" rhetoric down our throats? But our reality was sink or swim ... How about we meet and tell you more of our lived experiences?

Why didn't the Chief Nurse then, or the subsequent Chief Nurse, care about us and our development?

Why were none of us included in the Band 4 assessor roles that were created? Look at your provision and notice our exclusion then, let's talk ... frankly and honestly.'

Nsoramma: 'Your rhetoric and our lived experiences are worlds apart, have the courage to challenge institutional discrimination!'

Nsaa: 'Why did the CEO fail to keep his promise to Sankofa that he would correct our pay injustice?

Do you care that you have lost our trust, and would you agree that when trust is eroded it must be re-earned? We're open to talk, if you're open to LISTEN and HAVE THE COURAGE TO OVERSEE CHANGE!'

Finally, this is what we would like to say to mature Black sisters ... Aya and Akoma.

Akoma: 'Sorry, can I interject something here? This cultural approach is inspiring. Maya Angelou asserts:

> We may encounter many defeats, but we must not be defeated. It may be necessary to encounter defeats so we know who the hell we are, what we can overcome. What makes us stumble and fail and somehow miraculously rise and go on. (*The Late Show: Face to Face* 2006)

I needed to add that we are more than victims, we are moving on despite it all ... ok, go on, Aya.'

Aya: 'Be informed, so you can rise!'

Akoma: 'Research the courses you are offered and explore the promises prior to accepting your place.
Insist on getting ALL promises or assurances in writing.
Invest time in researching the history of your people in the context you will be working and studying.'

Aya: 'Be informed, so you can rise!'

Akoma: 'Be more than grateful, be in the know.
Be in the know about how you like to learn and ask for your preferred learning styles.
Be in the know about the relationships you want with mentors and coaches and hold each accountable to it.'

Aya: 'Be informed, so you can rise!'

Akoma: 'Be one who questions.
Be one who seeks out support.
Be one who uses her voice.
Be one who reads, widely, reading empowers and motivates. Reading may not come naturally either, reading will require discipline, read and reread until you understand then share.'

Aya: 'Be informed, so you can rise!'

Akoma: 'Be one who counts the cost before she starts, consider how you will build resilience as disappointments/setbacks will inevitably be part of your journey.
Be one who intentionally rises and goes on, in spite of the setbacks ... to your own development and to helping others on their way too.'

Owo: 'I love the cultural manifestation. My word ... bear with me whilst I appreciate the moment ... there is something to be said about not naming but interrogating and inviting dialogue. I loved the way you asked questions of the institutions rather than prescribe to them. Mama B, we need to have a conversation about that approach ... I, I really liked it, I really feel this. I, I just love this reciprocal learning space yet, I think this is a great place to end. I hope you all agree. Thanks for letting me in ... cherished it ... I hope to join you again, but as a sojourner.'

Sankofa: 'Ladies, I'm sure you would like to join me appreciating Owo for a stimulating and thought provoking session. Also, please give yourselves an applaud for pulling that presentation out of the bag with so little preparation time. Wow ... well done! Now remember our agreement, the final session will be held without me or Mama B and following that meeting, GyeNyame, your nominated spokesperson will let us know whether you wish to, and if you do, how you will proceed. In the meantime, I have the task of writing up our time in this space. Thank you and I look forward to hearing from you soon.'

The women hastily gather their belongings and make their way towards the exits.

SCENE 8

Sankofa's reflection and guidance

Sankofa arrives home exhausted but equally exhilarated, she puts away the bags and books. She changes into her yard clothes, sets up the coffee machine and heads off to the patio. She plans an all-nighter as she wants to capture as much of the session's reflections as she can whilst it is still fresh. She decides to take a short break so she lowers herself into the rocking chair. The garden is tranquil, the moon is full. Staring at the stars she slowly drifts into a state of semi-consciousness. As she drifts she dreams ...

A tiny, dark skinned, white haired, character appears. She is pencil thin with big eyes and lovely white teeth. She is draped in crisp Kente cloths and speaks with a quiet voice. She introduces herself as Akoko Nan. She explains that she is an ancestral parent and, in fact, that is exactly what her name means. She informs Sankofa that she has come to help her with her reflections on this leg of her journey.

Sankofa:	(Contemplatively.) 'What has it all been about?'
Akoko Nan:	'What, my child?'
Sankofa:	'This whole journey, you know my last half decade. Life, power, exploitation, superiority, inequalities, failure, inferiority, injustice, fear, silencing, subordination, life ... what is it all about?'
Akoko Nan:	'Tell me, my child, what have you found?'
Sankofa:	'Where do I start? How do I share it? What I have found is huge, not all new in the larger scheme of things, but new to me. Your question is too big for me. What have I found? Well, I have strove to reclaim our oral history whilst acknowledging that, because of navigating two cultures, that was not without challenge! I have written using an approach called autoethnography, and as Herrmann (2014) asserts:

> autoethnographies bridge the gap between the remembered past, the fleeting now, and the ephemeral here after. (p. 337)

I have relived the past, reviewed the present and I am leaving an account of our lived experiences for the future.

Our ancestors ... it's strange saying that now I am actually talking to you Akoko Nan ... you left us with positive examples of unified approaches to: community-empowerment, community education and self-definition.

Even under colonialism Black nurses were self-motivated, strategic and impressively effective in gaining equal professional status to whites and rising to the higher echelons of nursing in the Caribbean. Many of your ancestors were politically astute, you ancestors utilised constitutional change to work to your benefit. Many of you did not rely on white advocates.

I re-lived the challenges of the impact of British education on Black Caribbean immigrants and their children. I learnt a great deal about how two generations, our parents and our own, simultaneously struggled towards self-identity in Britain during the 1980s. To our credit, many of my generation can navigate British and Caribbean cultures seamlessly. Having said that, Black stereotypes are still used to keep us mute and in subordinated places in the workplace and the wider society.

The educational history of my generation in the UK is tainted, but inequitable educational experiences rallied us to educational proactivity, where we became co-educators through supplementary, self-funded politically active Saturday schools. But we haven't sustained our influence, historically, and to this day, nursing education has been problematic for way too many Black women, in that, it has not been an equitable provision.

Nursing reforms need more thorough consultation and intentional efforts to avoid knee jerk reactions which are strategically flawed, thus contributing to poor educational experiences and manpower waste. The Assistant Practitioner's role being an example of an under-utilised provision. Widening participation was a good concept in principle but not more than mere rhetoric in practice. Widening happened, but not much else changed ... Akoko Nan ... are you hearing to me?'

Akoko Nan: 'I'm hearing child ... continue ...'

Sankofa: 'Widening participation was problematic because the educational opportunity it offered was not transformative. Yes, there were a few examples of good practice, but sadly way too few! The university followed the "pattern of organisation" and their approaches were inflexible and inequitable.

Sankofa's reflection and guidance

In both the university and the workplace, structures and behavioural patterns reinforced a closed society of production and consumption. Unfortunately, the educational experiences of mature Black women presently are not significantly different from the education our parents experienced during colonialism.

I have learnt that the institutional structures are reliant on us being un-informed. If we remain ignorant we will always be conduits of exploitation. We need to break and keep on breaking our colonial mindsets. We must advocate and make critical thinking our normative approach. We must interrogate more and trust less. We must call to remembrance that the NHS, that called our parents because it was understaffed since 1948, still suffers the stigma and reality of not being able to retain nurses in our present time. We must engage with our history and be informed.

We need to cast off the labels and challenge the stereotypes imposed on us. We need to educate the nursing profession that they are "not doing us a favour". They need us, and to retain us, they need to respect us. We need to throw off our fear of mobilisation. For goodness sake, our parents travelled from the Caribbean. Sometimes we struggle to think about travelling within the county for work. Gosh, we need to wake up! ... Akoko Nan ... What are you thinking? Why are you silent? Please help me out?'

Akoko Nan: 'You are summarising what you have learnt my child ... do not get frustrated by my silence ... go on ...'

Sankofa: 'It was frustration and a refusal to remain silent that initially fuelled me to embark on this PhD journey. Purpose and passion sustained me. This journey has been phenomenal, I have learnt from the past, I am filled with excitement and anticipation about how this work will inform, inspire and educate future generations. Akoko Nan, anything to add?'

Akoko Nan: 'For the record my child ... I believed in you and I'm proud of you. Don't ever underestimate the force that drives you. Go on ...'

Sankofa: 'You did? You are? ... Thanks, that means so much to me! Now, the non-transformative education was not only experienced by Black British and Black Caribbean women. However, it was only the accounts of the Black women that were of interest to me, simply because in the context of the NHS we are generally written about, we don't write about ourselves. In one of our sessions we joked about dreamers and dreaming, but for me this dream was no joke, I felt compelled to see this through. Abdulai (1995) asserts:

Perseverance molds dreams into reality – above all, it is the only divide that separates the dream from the dreamer, and on which all ideas are molded into matter. Thus, not to persevere is to throw in the towel. (p. 64)

Akoko Nan, do you have any messages for us?'

Akoko Nan: 'Tradition would say, you should produce a list of recommendations, however, your work is not a traditional piece. Your work asks the readers, especially those in HEI, NHS and primarily Black women, to discuss and put in place processes to ensure that this generation is the last to be educationally SUBJUGATED and professionally EXPLOITED by the NHS. The women who completed the first year and exited have a partial qualification which can be completed at some time in the future.

We ancestors would have desired that all women complete the course, most education is good and transferable, but we understand, in our discussions we've accepted that what the women who stepped off the course in year one achieved was "Exploitation Escapism". Their plight was temporary, whilst they have life and there is hope, they can complete at some point in the future and rise professionally. However, my child, they need to invest in self-belief and self-empowerment, they need to learn to push past their minor insignificant differences and UNITE. Our children often rely on others to advocate for them because they think they are weak. Their weakness is in their separateness. United, and I do not just mean in numbers, but in spirit, in purpose and in the cause that is greater than each individually, they would be an influential force to be reckoned with.

The lack of historical knowledge is a deficit they can no longer entertain. They must engage. Knowledge empowers. I tell you this dear child, "not to know is bad, not to wish to know is worse". If only they could see, their ancestors were strong together, listen to them, go and learn from history, increase your awareness and listen to your intuition. My child, my own ancestors taught us that "if we stand tall, it is because we stand on the shoulders of many ancestors." My dear, I see you are tired, but I have an admonition for you, use this prose as you engage with our communities. You are primed for activism!

How can we know we don't know, if what we don't know, we ought to know and what we now know is "his-story"? But what we should know is "our-story". How can we tell "the-story" of "our-story" when "his-story" is now "our-story"? How can we even begin to tell "our-story"?

Do we then accept "his-story" as "our-story"? No, we cannot and should not, and ought not accept "his-story" as "our-story". Then to revisit our past we must. Then to revisit our past we must.
To reclaim "our-story" we are challenged.
To rewrite "our-story" for posterity is our task.
So abibiman Sankofa.
It's not a shame to revisit the past when you have forgotten.
Neither is it forbidden to learn from the past.
Neither is it taboo to emulate aspects of the past.
So "abibiman Sankofa".
Perhaps then, by consulting the past, we can create the future.
(Abdulai 1995: 49).

Sankofa: 'I'm proud of this project. It gives us a voice though, Gandin (2006) would argue:

> it is not that the subalterns are not speaking; voices are being raised, but mainstream discourses have constantly overpowered them. (p. 217)

This work encourages others to dialogue and hopefully respectfully listen. Workplaces and HE are fully aware, as Gandin (2006) again argues: "there are other ways to organise education and it is far from impossible to implement them" (p. 217). Education providers must choose to move away from the "one size fits all" approach to education and this discursive work is one of the "weapons" for deconstructing traditional approaches experienced by many minority groups.

It is important that we provide this counter argument to education providers as, in the words of Gandin (2006):

> the rhetoric of neoliberalism insists on the importance of education to solve the problems of capitalism ... yet education has failed to efficiently provide workers with the appropriate skills. (p. 219)

As I approach the closing of this reflection, I recall reading a piece from Carter-Black (2008) where she painted such a visualisation for me as she discussed her PhD journey. She said:

I was immediately immersed in a group of women with whom I would share a range of events and all the various and commensurate emotions. There was laughter, camaraderie and tears of joy. We shared almost unparalleled levels of anxiety, weariness, exhaustion and sheer unmitigated terror. At times, it seemed that we redefined the term stressed out. Huddled together, connected at the hip, we clawed our way through a process experienced by a very small percentage of the world's population – even smaller if you are a Black woman. (p. 118)

I longed for the opportunity of those shared experiences but I had to settle for the dream and the hope that not long from now, Carter-Black's lived experience will be many Black women's educational realities here in the UK. Transformative education should never be easy and for that very reason it should never be experienced in isolation. For me, it's been a very lonely journey ... I'm so tired, Akoko Nan, would you mind if I just stay here and sleep a while on your shoulders ... Black women's activism is ... the snooze is over.

(Sankofa awakes.)

Postscript

This ethnodrama with 'our' narratives and stories has been set in what is classified as the post-colonial, post-modernist paradigm. Bochner (2014) argues that autoethnography was birthed from thinking and questioning differently. He asks:

> Can my work achieve importance? Can it matter if our authors aren't willing to show their faces? Should one of the standards by which social science enquiry is judged be the extent to which readers feel the truth of our stories. So, seeking to open a space for this kind of enquiry ... (p. 4)

The Sankofa concept fuelled and sustained me throughout the years of this project. Sankofa means: 'go back, learn from the past, then move forward.' Autoethnography, as an approach to presenting our narratives, supported my aim to engage with the past so we can be wiser in the ways in which we respond to what institutions offer us, labelled as opportunities. Bochner (2014) posits:

> You can't bear the thought of losing the past or making it disappear as it did for your parents. The mission of all story tellers is to keep history alive but it's not your own it's the calling of all storytellers to go back and reclaim the past, pay attention this time, figure out what you can do with your stories, keep memory alive; make it meaningful. There is no reason to relive the past unless it can help you to anticipate the future. We seek a more just world in which to live. (p. 2)

The past has produced much learning about Black women's experiences primarily in the nursing profession within Britain's NHS. One of the most important lessons from the past has been the example of what Black women facing social, professional and structural injustices can accomplish when they become co-constructors of their liberation. Education with interconnectedness must be our ticket out of some of our personal, mental and institutional incarcerations. Black feminist stance offered the opportunity to make the voices of Black women the dominant voices, to unmute them, to centralise them, to listen to them and make sense with them.

The Assistant Practitioner's course has already been replaced by the Associate Nurse's programme. What this means for the current APs who are still seeking their band 4 position is not fully known. This work is unfinished, my commitment to social action and inclusion means that this is merely the end of this part of the journey. Koro-Ljungberg (2016) helps me to articulate my justification for not subscripting to a conventional ending, she asserts:

> Conclusions and endings are likely to imply the final word, complete stops and loss of beginnings. Rather than writing about concluding thoughts, I want to direct readers' attention to productive 'failures' of unfinished research, since without a conclusion I am failing to conclude my text, my thoughts. I also fail to provide you my readers a way out, a reason to stop reading, interacting and thinking ... Productive failure has to do with partiality and absence. Something about the research and researchers'/participants' interactions is still to come and to be continued and extended. (p. 101)

This book encourages readers to continue thinking about, equality, inclusion and fairness in our National Treasure. True inclusion requires us to make a shift from personal comfort and muting to curiosity, questioning and acting. The biggest barrier to true inclusion is mindset. Black people are not asking for special treatment; all we ask is for leaders and managers in the NHS to set and maintain working environments that will allow ALL people to thrive. Everyone deserves to be whatever they can achieve, all each of us need is a fair platform.

Bibliography

Abdulai, D. (1995). *Sankofa: Stories, Proverbs and Poems of an African Childhood.* Denver, CO: Eastwood Printing.
Apple, M. (2013). *Can Education Change Society.* New York: Routledge.
Baldwin, J. (1985). *Evidence of Things Not Seen.* New York: Henry Bolt and Co.
Ball, S. (2008). *The Education Debate.* Bristol: Policy Press.
Bathwater, A. (2010). Seamlessness or separation: negotiating further and higher education boundaries in dual sector institutions. *Improving Learning by Widening Participation in Higher Education.* Oxon: Routledge.
Baxter, C. (1998). *The Black Nurse: An Endangered Species.* A case for equal opportunities in nursing. Cambridge: National Extension College for Training in Health and Race.
Blair, T. (2005). *Monthly Press Conference.* 10 Downing Street, 24 October, in Hall.
Bochner, A. (2014). Celebrating the 10th anniversary of ICQI: Body, paper, stage of performance autoethnography as a way of social transformations: challenges and hopes speech. Tenth International Congress of Qualitative Inquiry May 21–24 (unpublished May 2014).
Bochner, A. (2014). *Coming to Narrative, A personal History of Paradigm Change in the Human Sciences.* Walnut Creek, CA: Left Coast Press.
Boylorn, R. (2013). *Sweetwater, Black Women and Narratives of Resilience.* New York: Peter Lang.
Boylorn, R. (2016). On Being at Home with Myself: Blackgirl Autoethnography as Research Praxis. *International Review of Qualitative Research.* 9(01), pp. 45–58.
Carter-Black (2008). A Black Woman's Journey into a Predominantly White Academic World. *Journal of Woman and Social Work.* 23(2), pp. 112–122.
Collins, J. M. (2015). *250 Years and Still a Slave – Breaking Free with Active Centralised Empowerment*: A New Way of Thinking and Performing. Charleston, IL: Visionary Insight Press.
Davis, A. (1988), in Yancey, G., *African American Philosophers – 17 Conversations.* New York: Routledge.
Dei, G. J. (2010). *Fanon and the Counterinsurgency of Education.* Boston, MA: Sense Publishers.
Dewey, J. (1997). *Experience and Education*: *The Kappa Delta Pi Lecture Series.* New York: Touchstone.

Dubois, W. E. B. (1973). *The Education of Black People. Ten Critiques, 1906–1960*. New York: Monthly Review Press.

Fanon, F. (1967). *Black Skins, White Masks*. New York: Grove Press.

Freire, P. (1974). *Education for Critical Consciousness*. London: Continuum.

Freire, P., and Macedo, D. (1987). *Literacy, Reading the Word and the World*. South Hadley, MA: Bergin and Garvey Publishers.

Gandin, L. (2006). Creating Real Alternatives to Neoliberal Policies in Education: The Citizen School Project. In M. W. Apple and K. L. Buras (eds) (2006), *The Subaltern Speak: Curriculum, Power and Educational Struggles*. Routledge: Oxon.

Giroux, H. (1987). Critical theory and the politics of culture and voice: Rethinking the discourse of educational research. In R. Sherman and R. Webb (eds), *Qualitative Research in Education: Focus and Methods*. New York: Falmer.

Harris, L. (1988), in Yancey, G. *African American Philosophers – 17 Conversations*. New York: Routledge.

Herrmann, A. (2014). The Undead as Autoethnographic Bridges. *International Review of Qualitative Research* 7(03), pp. 327–341.

Hill-Collins, P. (1991) *Black Feminist Thought. Knowledge, Consciousness and the Politics of empowerment*. New York: Routledge.

Hockings, C., Cooke, S., and Bowl, M. (2010). Pedagogies for social diversity and difference. In M. David (ed.), *Improving Learning by Widening Participation in Higher Education*. Oxon: Routledge.

hooks, b. (1981). *Ain't I a woman: Black Women and Feminism*. London: Pluto Classics.

Imbo, S. O. (2001). *Oral Traditions as Philosophy: Okot p'Bitek's Legacy for African Philosophy*. New York: Rowman & Littlefield.

Jones, S. H., Adams, T. E., and Ellis, C. (eds) (2013). *Handbook of Autoethnography*. Walnut Creek, CA: Left Coast Press.

Koro-Ljungberge, M. (2016). *Reconceptualizing Qualitative Research: Methodologies without Methodology*. Los Angeles, CA: Sage.

Lorde, A. (2007). *Sister Outsider*. New York: Crossing Press Inc.

Piper, A. (1998), in Yancey, G. African *American Philosophers – 17 Conversations*. New York: Routledge.

Reay, D., Ball, S., and David, M. (2010). It's Taking Me a Long Time but I'll Get There in the End: Mature students on access courses and higher education choice. *British Educational Research Journal* 28(1), pp. 5–19.

Tuwe, K. (2016). The African Oral Tradition Paradigm of Storytelling as a Methodological Frameworks: Employment experiences for African ... in New Zealand. Proceedings of the 38th AFSAAP Conference: 21st Century Tensions and Transformation in Africa, Deakin University, 28–30 October 2015 (Published February 2016).

Bibliography

West, C. (1982). *Prophecy Deliverance – An Afro American Revolutionary Christianity*. Philadelphia, PA: Westminster Press.

West, C. (1988), in Yancey, G. African *American Philosophers – 17 Conversations*. New York: Routledge.

Woodson, C. G. (1933) *The Mis-education of the Negro*. New York: The Associated Publishers.

Yancey, G. (1998) *African American Philosophers – 17 Conversations*. New York: Routledge.

Songs

Cliff, J. (1969). 'Many Rivers to Cross'. Trojan Records.
Herman, J. (1983). 'I am what I am'. [CD]
Marley, R. (1980). 'Redemption Song'. [CD] Island Tuff Gong
Rucker, D. (2010). 'This'. [CD] Capitol: Nashville.
The Hollies (1969). 'He ain't heavy, he's my brother'. Parlophone, Epic.

Poems and prose

Adams, N. (2013). Prayer. <http://www.goddessblogs.com/2013/09/a-meditation-on-achieving-human.html>

'Success' from 'The Ladder of Saint Augustine' by Henry Wadsworth Longfellow (1807–1882) <http://holyjoe.org/poetry/longfellow1.htm>.

Williamson, M. (1975). 'Our deepest fear'. <http://skdesigns.com/internet/articles/quotes/williamson/our_deepest_fear>.

Index

affective equality 55, 59, 66
Assistant Practitioner 43, 110, 116
autoethnography 3, 109, 115, 117

Black British, Caribbean 1, 2, 29, 111
Black Feminist stance, epistemologies 2, 3, 15, 24, 115

deficit theory model 3
dialectical conversations 29

engaged pedagogy 60, 100

foundation degree 14, 19, 29

hegemony 2, 24, 26

ontology 25, 87

oral accounts, storytelling, testimonies 2, 3, 9

pattern of organisation 67, 110
professional development 1, 98

resilience 18, 68, 75, 83

Sankofa 1, 59, 115

theoretical framework 3
transformative education 25, 68, 111, 114
Tuskegee Experiment 31

West, Cornel 24, 25, 40, 99, 100
widening participation 13, 26, 52, 55, 60, 74, 110
work-based learning 14, 36, 55, 71, 78, 98, 100, 104